© Andy Orrick

ABOUT THE AUTHOR

JULIAN RIDGWAY was born in Leicester, England. An Oxford graduate and a veteran of at least a dozen bands, he now researches rock photographs, writes for a host of magazines, and lives in London.

BANDALISM

BANDALISM

The Rock Group Survival Guide

JULIAN RIDGWAY

HARPER

ENTERTAINMENT

An Imprint of HarperCollinsPublishers

HARPER ● ENTERTAINMENT

HarperCollins books may be purchased for educational, business, or sales promotional use. For information please write: Special Markets Department, HarperCollins Publishers, 10 East 53rd Street, New York, NY 10022.

FIRST U.S. EDITION

Designed by Justin Dodd

Library of Congress Cataloguing-in-Publication Data is available upon request.

ISBN 978-0-06-164559-4

08 09 10 11 12 ID/RRD 10 9 8 7 6 5 4 3 2 1

TO GERRY

bandalism [**ban**-dᵊl-i-zəm] *n.*: the willful or malicious destruction of, or damage to, the fabric of a rock/pop/indie group brought about by one or more of its members

CONTENTS

LIST OF ILLUSTRATIONS   XI

PREFACE—"OH, YOU'RE IN A BAND? YOU ANY GOOD?"   XIII

1—THE RIGHT BAND   1

Chemistry   1

Band Members–What You're Looking For   4

Who Plays What–The Personality Test   20

Your Answers—The Personality Types   28

Crossbreeds   33

The Results   43

2—GETTING IT TOGETHER   51

Getting to Know Each Other   52

Rehearsing   56

The Heart-Head Horseshoe   59

The Band Types   61

The Rehersal Methods   66

Rehersal Tips   80

Finding an Image   87

Finding a Name   93

3—THE FIRST ALBUM   99

    Checking Your MySpace Page   100
    The Music Industry Igloo   104
    The First Album   120
    Promotion   125
    Touring   137

4—THE DIFFICULT SECOND ALBUM, AND BEYOND   151

    Sex, Drugs, and Rock 'n' Roll   153
    The Horoscopes   154
    Firing People   164
    Trouble at the Top   168
    At Last . . . the Difficult Second Album   175
    And Beyond . . .   186

5—BREAKING UP IS SO VERY HARD TO DO   189

    The Healthy Band Checklist   190
    The Life Cycle of a Band   192
    Snap Out of It   195
    There's Still a Chance   200
    After the Band Has Gone   214
    So Is It Finally Time   221

SUMMARY—SO WHAT HAVE WE LEARNED OVERALL?   227

THE BANDALISM HELP DESK   229

LIST OF ILLUSTRATIONS

Fig. 1: The Best Way to Find Band Members   15

Fig. 2: The Bandalistic Personality Test   23

Fig. 3–7: Troubleshooting Charts   45–49

Fig. 8: The Bandalistic Bonding Questionnaire   55

Fig. 9: The Heart-Head Horseshoe   60

Fig. 10: www.myspace.com/abandofbassplayers   102

Fig. 11: The Music Industry Igloo   105

Fig. 12: The Bryan Ferry Self-Diagnosis Thermometer   146

Fig. 13: The Firing Spiral   166

Fig. 14: Second Album Venn Diagram   181

Fig. 15: The Healthy Band Checklist   191

Fig. 16: The Life Cycle of a Band   193

Fig. 17: The Break-Up Zone (Detail)   194

PREFACE

"OH, YOU'RE IN A BAND? YOU ANY GOOD?"

"No. We spend all our time in rehearsals arguing about pointless drum fills and hating on famous bands for being shit. And when we're not doing that, we're just sitting in a bar shouting about how fucking amazing our new song is to our bored friends (whom we fully intend to ditch when we're famous) even though at the minute it's just half a chorus and we secretly know it's a bit shakey and completely ripped off from a U2 song. We haven't really got a bass player because everyone who responds to our ads is a wanker and we haven't played a gig since September last year. Not one person we don't know personally has ever said a single complimentary word about us."

"Yeah, we're fucking awesome, man—check out our My-Space."

Bands are stupid. Bands are deluded. And bands are seemingly hell-bent on making exactly the same mistakes as every other band in history time and time again. Which is why most bands are rubbish and why even the great ones usually go spectacularly off the rails long before they get anywhere near achieving their real musical potential. This is bandalism—the obsession bands appear to have with self-harming.

"Yeah *other* bands maybe," you sniff haughtily, "not ours! We're not stupid. Believe me, we know what we're doing."

Really? I'd bet a substantial sum of money that you're heading toward just the same messy oblivion as the rest. Because most bands, while they may be outlaws bound for hell or glory on the rock 'n' roll highway, are peculiarly conservative when it comes to following the Department of Rock 'n' Roll's Highway Code:

- You must fail to look after yourself
- You must screw up your songwriting with self-indulgent laziness
- You must behave like children
- You must fail to communicate with each other properly and fall out
- You must make a rubbish second album and then continue to get worse until your merciful demise

And I've had enough, frankly. Enough of this idiot's doctrine of self-fulfilling doom. It doesn't create mystique, it creates misery. I've heard it parroted by producers, managers, journalists, and lots of other people who should know better. Then I've seen it lived out by bands who . . . well . . . probably shouldn't. It's lazy nonsense and it destroys bands. And bands make some of my favorite music. So, obviously enough, I hate being continually disappointed by them and seeing them self-destruct. I'm not trying to make you boring. The very opposite—I want you to have an interesting story all of your own. Not the same half-finished one as all but about twenty other bands in history.

The point of this book is simple then: to reveal the mistakes so your band doesn't have to make them too.

Starting with how to form the right band, ending with when to break up, and taking in all the normal pitfalls along the way—how to rehearse, how to find an image, how to bond, how to deal with gigs, recording, the press, record companies, fans, disgruntled partners, drugs, tension, rivalry, touring, falling out, madness, firings, addictions, and, of course, how to make the Difficult Second Album—all without breaking up for stupid reasons. It will also help you answer the crucial questions of the rock 'n' roll universe, like, "What is 'nervous exhaustion' and how do you avoid it?" or "What's actually in it for the bass player?"

So now there is no excuse. If you follow the advice of this book, you will be doing everything in your power to avoid bandalism. To avoid being just another shit band—clogging up crappy venues with your uninspired, derivative musical slurry, getting a lucky break, fucking it all up, and ending up shunting shopping carts around a parking lot, or data around a database, with nothing to show for your twenties but press clippings, alcoholism, bitterness, and lots of unsold copies of your third single. Instead you will change musical history, change the world, and avoid going mad or dying in the process. So shut up and read.

BANDALISM

1

THE RIGHT BAND

The starting point in your anti-bandalism quest is, obviously enough, to form the right band in the first place. If you construct the right band from the start you are instantly removing some of the pressures of disintegration. But what is the right band? There are hundreds of different types of music you could be playing (or at least ten). Hundreds of different bands have been put together with thousands of different members. How can there be any such thing as a "right" band? How can you form it? What are you looking for? Good players? Good people to spend hours of your life hanging around with? People with loads of friends they can bring to gigs with them? Well, all of those. Sort of. But there's one more crucial ingredient . . .

Chemistry

It doesn't matter what sort of band you're forming, you have to have the right chemistry between you—the feeling that this collection of people is special, or that you're somehow on the same wavelength and going somewhere exciting. If you want to form a brilliant band, it has to feel like there's some bond of potential, some kind of shared and wonderful future that only you can have. Some of the time anyway.

Chemistry, though, is a very silly word. It's like "beautiful." A catch-all term people use to describe something they can't explain. Unfortunately it's the word great bands themselves most often choose to describe what makes them so effortlessly wonderful. Which is a bit of a shame, as having a more specific term available might be quite useful. Seeing as it's so important and everything.

Usually it rears its head when bands say things like, "We started playing and we just *knew* we had something special—this kind of chemistry." Does this mean people in great bands are just gifted with magical self-confidence? If you don't go around just *knowing* things all the time should you give up and do something more sensible with your life? Something with qualifications and things? Are people in great bands specially chosen ones whose works humble mortals emulate at their peril?

It seems unlikely. If this was the case, why is the history of rock 'n' roll littered with the rotting carcasses of terrible journeyman second albums, or bands that spend their whole careers getting incrementally less interesting? No, people in great bands are not Gods set among us (Johnny Borrell* take note). They are ordinary people who got it right. Usually, just ordinary people who get it right for a bit then mess it all up. But when they get to tell the world about their band and its luminous interpersonal chemistry in interviews they are at the peak of fame. Nosefuls of hubris and a disorientating series of slaps on the back leave them with a temporary amnesia to

---

* Singer for Razorlight.

all the hundreds of times along the way they sat round thinking, "Yeah, but are we actually just shit?" Oh no, by then they just *knew* all along.

So is it all utter nonsense? Is there no such thing as chemistry? Is it, like Santa Claus and social mobility, a beguiling abstraction dangled in front of us when we start asking too many questions? Is it instead closer to the truth to say that any band will do—that being a great band is more about a bit of hard work than this teasing phantom "chemistry"?

No. Sorry. Hard work helps and everything (it's pretty much essential), but great bands do just feel right. Great bands make the members feel, however much they may love or despise one another, that this is *the* band. It is this that marks them out from mediocre ones, and without it, you're wasting your time.

"Okay! What is it then?" you scream. Erm, well it's a bit tricky to explain. Like love, it comes in many forms but you know when you've got the real thing. Also like love, in most cases you don't have it but are deluding yourself to make life feel less hopeless. And again like love, it's very, very hard to define. But if we can't prescribe it, we can at least diagnose it. Here are five telltale signs your band has chemistry and five that say it doesn't:

Chemistry

1. You can't stop smiling after rehearsals
2. You don't want the songs to end when you're playing
3. You feel like you're doing something new
4. You look round the room and the rest of the band looks really cool
5. You actually sound good and people like you with little persuasion

No Chemistry

1. You begin rehearsals hoping that the bass player won't turn up so you can knock off early
2. You know exactly how many carpet tiles there are on the floor of the rehearsal room
3. You believe it will all somehow click when you've been playing together for a couple more months
4. You wish the drummer wouldn't do that
5. You never tell your friends when you're playing gigs

If you're already in the first category, you have chemistry, so move right along to the next section, "Who Plays What." If you're in the second—and now you really *have* to be honest—it's time to form another band. And quickly. Think of how many bands you like that had made it by the time they were your age. This time it needs chemistry. And that means finding the right people.

Luckily, you are only looking for one of three things in a band member. And just in case you aren't so liberally buttered with self-belief that you know already, here's what you're after:

Band Members—What You're Looking For

1. You Like Them

The easiest of the lot. They just seem okay. You get on with them. They're the right sort of person. But how do you know if you like them? Actually, that's getting silly. You have friends, don't you? I can't do everything for you. Do you want me to come over and write the songs too? It doesn't really matter why you like them. Though in the case of bands, it's probably because they're a bit like you. It might seem like this criterion fits "nice" bands the best. It's unlikely that a violent hardcore band would lay as much stress on something as lame as liking someone as would, say, a delicate, pigeon-toed jangly indie band. But that depends on your definition of "like." You might "like" being with aggressive people who pay scant regard to personal hygiene and social etiquette. I'm not here to define all the parameters of taste. Sadly.

Liking someone is the quickest and most painless way of getting them in the band. Sixties mod pop midgets the Small Faces recruited keyboard player Ian McLagan on this basis. He had just left his previous band (on the off-ramp of a motorway arguing over a broken down van) and, looking for work, had been invited to the offices of old-school showbiz hustler Don Arden to meet one of his acts. The act in question, the Small Faces, were, at the time, trying to get rid of their keyboard player Jimmy Winston for his twin sins of being too tall and showing off too much when they appeared on telly. McLagan and the band had never met, but as singer Steve Marriott recalled, when he walked in the room, "Here's a guy, standing right in front of us, who was already one of the boys. The chemistry between us was perfect . . . his humor was perfect, his charisma was perfect—all I could do was hug him."

Ah! So something was definitely right. At this point they hadn't even heard him play. He could have been rubbish. But that didn't really matter because they liked him. He seemed to fit in. Jarvis Cocker tells a similar, though suitably dead-pan, tale about finding Pulp's drummer. On the way to Nick Banks's first rehearsal with the group, Jarvis got followed home by a bull terrier. Before he'd even sat down at his kit, Banks was pressed into service, wandering round the Sheffield suburbs with him trying to lose the dog. "During the course of walking around," recalled Jarvis, "we talked and got on well, so we thought we'd have him. We'd never heard him play the drums and certainly wouldn't have if we had." There is an important lesson here. Being good at playing an instrument is of far less importance than being the right person to fit in with the band.*

And if Pulp's tale sounds suitably northern and down-to-earth, Joy Division's positively reeks of dour, drizzly anti-glamour. Bernard Sumner took on doomed poet of gloom Ian Curtis as the band's singer because, he said, "I knew he was all right to get on with and that's what we based the whole group on. If we liked someone they were in."

So the simple first step is to go for people because you like them. Which, while it might seem blindingly obvious, probably cuts out about 80 percent of potential band members straight away. After all, as you probably already know, people in bands are picky little bastards.

2. You Like Something About Them

You may not want to run up and hug them. Inside you may even be voicing grave misgivings about them. But there's still something about them you like. Maybe it's the fact they have a really good amp and you want to use it. Or they know some guy who can get you free rehearsal time. Or they have loads of good-looking friends whom you can get to come out to gigs. Perhaps they just have an amusing haircut. For whatever reason, though, there is something about them that would be useful for the band. Something you don't already have. There is sometimes little to separate the interpersonal chemistry of a great band from the behavior of cold-hearted mercenaries.†

---

* Cynics might also note another lesson—singers make a lot of the decisions then say "we" to cover it up.

† Like the wonderful scene in *Slade in Flame*, probably the finest film ever made about rock bands, when the fictitious Flame (played by Slade) ask their old drummer to be the roadie—"You just want me van," he replies. "You only wanted me to be your drummer 'cos you fancied me sister."

Maybe you just like their attitude. Smiths' guitarist Johnny Marr was convinced by drummer Mike Joyce not because of his rudimentary paradiddles or sparkling conversation, but because he turned up to his audition absolutely off his face on magic mushrooms. This apparently showed "balls" (and not lackadaisical unprofessionalism) and so Joyce became a Smith (or thought he did—a slight misunderstanding the High Court in London was left to sort out twenty years later. He was hired at least, though).

It can be something very trivial indeed. There is a very possibly apocryphal story that Adam Clayton got into U2 on the strength of his bright yellow curly hair rather than his bass playing. And a pretty face rarely goes amiss. Look at T. Rex. Marc Bolan ditched perfectly accomplished bongo player Steve Peregrin Took for the more camera friendly Mickey Finn, after realizing that being a huge pop star might be a far more lucrative occupation than being in John Peel's favorite band. Finn's questionable percussive talents and striking features were no hindrance to this revised plan for world domination. Especially as they were accompanied by a pliable, easy-going nature.

Sometimes there is nothing like a bit of mutual necessity for sharpening up a band's ability to get on. As long as the band needs the member and the member needs the band, the wheels of creativity tend to turn more smoothly. But don't let that lead you into the biggest trap of all. There is one thing that is never enough to like about a band member—that they happen to play the right instrument. Apart from the drums, learning the instruments most commonly found in a rock band is really easy. Getting the right person and teaching them to play doesn't take very long. It's also far better for a band to learn them together. Otherwise, the virtuosos among you will ruin all of your songs with tedious technical competence while the others just look on.*

So even if someone plays bass and you need a bass player, if you can't find anything else you like about them, stop answering your phone or pretend the band has split up. Being able to play the right instrument is of no importance. The same goes if you are vetting a potential band to join. Just wanting to be in any band for the sake of it is a truly shit idea. There are better things to give up your Sunday afternoons to. Even watching *Antiques Roadshow* or drinking alone in the park.

3. You Like Something About Playing with Them

So what about all those brilliant bands where all the members hate each other's guts then, you ask? They have spark and chemistry without having to be so bloody nice about everything all the time. They don't need to look desperately for self-definition from their insular little gang. They just turn up, hate each other, play some incendiary music, glower, have a great big fist fight, and then fuck off again. Yay! That's cool.

> Rock bands are generally miserable people. I knew my
> rock 'n' roll history. You didn't have to get along, that
> was a "hippy" ideal. Rock 'n' roll's about a bunch of
> ambivalent people getting together, hating each other,
> and playing loud, nasty, hateful music.
>
> —*J Mascis of Dinosaur Jr.*

---

* As a rough guide—an hour for super-basic keyboards, a week for simple bass, and an intensive month for basic rhythm guitar. Even drums don't have to be that hard. By Julian Cope's account, it took Teardrop Explodes drummer Gary Dwyer "about four weeks" to get good. The more you care, the more you are prepared to practice and make your hands bleed and the easier it gets.

So yes, there is always the Mascis model. And it can really work for some bands. All the personal tensions between members find an outlet in the music, meaning that however badly they all get on, something really works when they play together. It's certainly a far better situation than just having lukewarm, nothingy feelings about each other. If the band doesn't matter to you all that much, it's unlikely it will engage anyone else. But do remember that bands make things up and exaggerate all the time. At best, they love shrouding everything they do in myth (J Mascis won't even tell us what his first name is). One two-minute argument can easily get blown up into a bitter six-year feud—full of tense psychological melodrama and extreme violence—once the journalist's tape recorder is going and the band has a chance to show off just how dysfunctional they are.

But it is still true that the excitement of playing together is all many good bands have needed—excitement that might be more about picking fights through riffs than sharing harmonious musical epiphanies.[*] "Personal arguments carried out musically," as Mat Osman of Suede put it about the fractious early-nineties lineup of that band. "It was the sort of thing that four well-balanced human beings would probably have sorted out with an evening down the pub." What a good thing they weren't and they didn't.

Obviously it depends on whether you want to be the sort of band that keeps plodding along forever or one that melts down as quickly as it began, leaving only the debris of smashed personalities and rock 'n' roll carnage. Neither is better, as long as both create brilliant music. And secretly fantasizing that the drum skin is the singer's face is not in itself the secret to being a great band. This

---

[*] The Who got on so badly in their early days that they couldn't even bear to stay in the same room long enough for photographer Colin Jones to set his lights up when he took his iconic early portrait of the band.

third category is here to point out that *only* getting on musically won't stop you from being a great band. The band of brothers myth is not for everyone.

Likewise, even bands that come together using the first two methods still need to be excited by playing together. However much you like the other people in the room, if you're drifting off in the middle of a song wondering what you might like for dinner, it's probably time to think about leafing through the ads in the back pages of the *NME*.

How to Find the Right Members

Musicians Wanted Ads

Which brings us rather neatly to the tricky part. It's all very well knowing what to look for in band members, but where do you look? Where can you find those creatures whose entire life was a meaningless void until they joined your band? The back of the *NME*? New band websites? Crumpled ads by the door in guitar shops, complete with sadly expectant tear-off phone number strips along the bottom?

Picture the scene if you will. You get a call from a bass player who's seen your ad. You both love Dylan, though admittedly you haven't actually heard the songs he mentioned. Oh and he also went on about Charlie Mingus or something. But never mind. "Now we can take over the world!" you mutter to yourself as you finish the call. Wednesday evening arrives. You set up your stuff amid the scent of sickly amplifiers and half-finished joints left behind by the last band, in a dank room in the corner of a bleak industrial estate (when Bruce Springsteen came up with the expression *Darkness on the Edge of Town* he was surely thinking of cheap practice rooms). In walks a fifty-year old man in stonewashed jeans with an ironed-in crease. You mumble guarded pleasantries as he pulls out his shiny black headless bass. After handing over a bit of paper with the chords scribbled on it, the drummer counts in and the song stumbles to life. All eyes turn to the corner where a sludgy jazzy mess is creeping out of the crackly rented bass amp. Your world, your dreams, and everything that has kept you going since the age of fifteen through each shitty day on this godforsaken planet crumbles away sadly into the floor, amid your scribbled lyric sheets and distortion pedals.

So what are you doing wrong? Why is it only people like *that* reply to your ads? There are many times in the life of a band that are fearsomely depressing. But few are more so than flirting with the musicians wanted ads. This is because, like most things band-related, they are veiled with vagueness and half-truths. These ads are written in their own special language—one of hedged bets and flawed ambition. A quick look through a few shows why they so often turn up such wildly inappropriate people:

```
Versatile drummer needed urgently for
ambitious London band. Major label interest!
Gigs waiting. Infl. U2, Radiohead . . .
```

Most musicians wanted ads sound very, very boring indeed. And when they don't, they sound desperate. Sprinkled with a handful of bleakly echoing exclamation marks or peppered with pushy rhetoric—"must be committed," "must have ambition," "no time-wasters." Aaaarrrgggggh! GO AWAY! It's not a fucking sport! It's not like you're paying anything either. No wonder the last drummer left you if this is what you're like all the time. No. NO. NO! Ads use words like "dedicated" and "versatile." No one uses words like that about music. Not even Sting. And would you want to be in a band with people who actually did?

Then there are the lies. "Major label interest" means anything from "the guitarist's sister used to know a guy who worked at Warner," to "we e-mailed a link to our MySpace page unsolicited to three A&R men and got an out-of-office auto-reply from one of them." It does not mean that a major record company is interested in signing this band. It never means that. "Single deal!" means that the band has had a hundred CDs made and nearly got one stocked in the Rough Trade shop. Nearly in the sense that they haven't actually asked yet because it's always the scary guy working there when they go in and they don't dare. And we all know it. Great potential members aren't taken in by the patter. They just don't call. If they're really sensible, they weren't even reading.

And what about the desperation. "Gigs waiting." So why did you bother booking them when you hadn't actually got the band together yet? Surely they will be terrible.

```
Band with no dignity or professional
standards requires like-minded no-hoper
to go through the indie/rock/pop motions
with them in front of three of their bored
friends on a rainy Tuesday night every
month or so. No memorable songs or ideas.
Influences: stuff from about three years ago
and doomed self-delusion.
```

Oh yes, influences. A very useful thing you might think. Pop your influences down and you'll only get people who "dig" your "vibe." But that depends on a band being honest about the artists they like and sound like. And bands writing musicians wanted ads seem allergic to this common-sense precaution. Instead, a popular trick is for bands to list artists everybody likes. Which is very stupid. The point of the ad is to find someone who peculiarly fits into your band, not to have stilted telephone conversations with every unemployed keyboard player in the area. But even a more interesting list can be a risk. Do you *really* sound like Can? Thought not.

So in the end, the influences list usually means either "the three artists we're proudest of owning records by" or "these are the only three artists that all of us can agree we don't hate." Which is why, at time of writing, Dylan, Neil Young, REM, U2, Radiohead, the Beatles, the Stones, Nick Drake, Jeff Buckley, Joy Division, and Gang of Four make up 98 percent of artists listed in band ads. Bringing us back round to the start of the influences vicious circle.

So better not to list influences then? Sadly, no. That just leads to filling up the ad's word count with broad genre categories like "indie pop/rock" or, even worse, grabbing at impenetrable gibberish. As proof, here are some actual examples from the actual pages of the last few months' actual *NMEs*: "Music is intelligent and interesting." Interesting? That's alarmingly euphemistic. If someone tells you something and you say, "Oh, that's interesting," you mean you don't care, weren't listening, and never want to hear it again. Someone with an interesting face is ugly. It doesn't sound good. And intelligent? Come on, that's the compliment you pay when no others are available. Then how about the wonderful, "Must be talented but simple," or the eager and off-putting, "Open mind and free spirit essential." Free spirit? It sounds like a car ad. People genuinely wrote these things hoping it would lead to them forming a brilliant band. I would suspect it didn't work.*

So what does all this mean? That the only thing worth saying in one of these ads is:

```
Drummer wanted. No twats. Call if you're
interested and we'll go for a drink or
something.
```

In other words, the only thing you can realistically try and get from a musicians wanted ad is someone who plays the right instrument. Which is the quickest way to form a rubbish and pointless band. The very thing I'm trying to help you avoid. So in short, or rather at some ranting length, this method is a waste of time.

Other Methods (Ones That Are Actually Worth Doing)
So it seems we're back to square one again. How do you find the right people to be in the band? A quick consultation of the history books provides some helpful tips. And all these methods are far more fun and far, far less likely to lead to abject despair than the dreaded ads. I have put them in a convenient pie chart (*see Fig. 1, p. 15*) to make them easier on the eye.

This should hopefully make things a bit simpler. Maybe start with the most popular method and work your way down. As you can no doubt see, slaving over the right text for an ad is statistical idiocy. Great bands are great bands because they somehow project a core identity. They all look like they're part of one multiheaded beast.

---

* If you recognize these quotes and have since sold millions of albums, please let me know.

Figure 1. The Best Way to Find Band Members

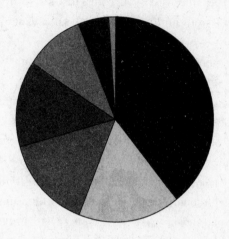

■ Friends and Acquaintances (38%)

■ Relatives (18%)

■ Poaching from Other Bands (15%)

■ Chance Meetings and Weird Accidents (14%)

■ Lovers (9%)

■ Obsessive Fans (6%)

■ Musicians Wanted Ads (1%)

We like them as fans because we'd secretly, or even not very secretly, like to be in the band too. You might be able to create that with a complete stranger who also likes commitment, dedication, and three really popular old bands, but to be honest, it sounds a bit far-fetched. Especially when you could just get your girlfriend to learn bass, make your brother buy a drum kit, and actually enjoy it all instead.

Of course, most bands form through a combination of these methods. For some, like Radiohead, it's delightfully simple. They all went to the same school and used to jam in the music room on Fridays (hence their terrible early name On a Friday). They even got a pair of brothers in too to make it all look deceptively easy.

At the other end of the scale, forming Belle and Sebastian took considerable ingenuity and enterprise from singer/guitarist/songwriter Stuart Murdoch. He had connections with a music business course whose participants were required to record and release an album by an unknown local artist. When his songs were picked for the project he needed to find a band to play them. He did that by hanging around an open mic night in a late-night café in Glasgow, asking all the people he liked the look of.

But both bands have something important in common. They show that one of the best ways to find people for your band is just to look around whatever room you happen to be in, tap whoever happens to be there on the shoulder and ask them. That also makes for a good story. Which means, later on, journalists will be nicer about you as you'll have done half of their work for them.

WHERE TO LOOK

Siblings and relatives are often a good place to begin. They won't be too shocked when your vicious spoiled brat side comes out in rehearsals. They have put up with your emotionally stunted behavior for their entire lives. You can't shock them now just because you've put a guitar on. Also there's no need to worry about offending them. Is telling them that they're singing flat really crueler than the time you made them eat slugs? With any luck it might provide a bit of rivalry and tension too. Sibling scuffles are great press.

But aside from the Oasis and Kinks models there are quieter examples of families in bands. Angus and Malcolm Young have plodded away together in AC/DC for over thirty years. More recently, Barry Hyde's little brother came in very useful when the Futureheads were short of a drummer. And of course the Magic Numbers take it to a tidy extreme as two brother/sister pairs. Actually, family bands have been especially popular over the last few years. The Mystery Jets even have the singer's dad in the band.

But not everyone wants to spend their every waking hour with people who share most of their DNA. That's what many people form bands to get away from. So what about the person you're hooking up with? Tim Gane muscled his girlfriend Laetitia Sadier into his band, McCarthy, before the pair decided to go off and form one of their own. Even having a child together didn't dim their enthusiasm for band life. They are still the core of Stereolab twenty years later. Sonic Youth and Blondie have also both managed to navigate long careers (albeit with a twelve-year gap in Blondie's case) despite or because of forming around couples.

If even that sounds far too intense and unhealthy, you could just try friends and acquaintances. Here it pays to keep your eyes open. There are numerous bands formed around close friendships—the Libertines being a more obvious recent example of buddies forming a very good band (their problem was that they didn't read the rest of this book . . .). But intense, dysfunctional blood-brother bonds are not everyone's cup of tea.* Especially if you're only looking for a drummer. Then you might just need to look around at the people you barely know at all.

Coldplay used most permutations of the "knowing people" method to find their lineup. Chris Martin and guitarist Jonny Buckland became close friends at university, started writing songs, and decided to form a band. Bassist Guy Berryman then accosted them in the student union bar and demanded to join (they say he was quite threatening about it, but somehow I don't believe that). This left them stuck for a drummer. And beware, this part of the story is very, very, very Coldplay. Chris Martin was moaning about their situation to a friend on his university hockey team. See, I warned you. This friend happened to live with a drummer and so they arranged an audition. But though mutual friend and drum kit arrived, the drummer didn't show up. Despite being a guitarist, the friend, Will Champion, had a bash on the kit and Coldplay was complete. Apart from the bit where he got kicked out for a couple of weeks after they got signed, he has been the drummer ever since. If they had been more picky about finding a proper drummer—one who had ever played before—they would probably have headed down to the pub and would now all be bitter academics or teachers at minor public schools, not huge pop stars. When looking for band members, it always pays to look at what's right under your nose.†

That's what happened to the Ramones too. Tom Erdelyi was a friend of the band who happened to play the drums. He helped them out when they were auditioning for drummers by demonstrating the parts to the potential Ramone recruits. Somehow it took

---

* Just look how it turned out for the Libertines.
† By the way, is it just me who wonders whether Will's "friend" actually existed?

them a while to notice that there was a drummer kicking about who knew them, and all their songs, and already enjoyed playing with them. But eventually common sense intervened and he became Tommy Ramone. Even in a band as carefully contrived as Roxy Music, Phil Manzanera was just helping out as sound engineer on their demos until their guitarist dropped out and they realized he was actually rather skillfull himself.[*]

So, seemingly, being in the right place at the right time and knowing it is the most reliable way of finding a suitable band member. The most famous tale of all is probably the meeting of Mick Jagger and Keith Richards that led to the formation of the Rolling Stones. They had known each other as children, but were reacquainted at a train station when Mick spotted the big pile of blues records Keith had tucked under his arm and went over for a chat.[†]

But for those who thumb their noses at chance and luck on the journey to form the perfect band, there's still no need to resort to the sorry small ads. There are always using and poaching left to try. Sick of tooling around in mediocre bands, Johnny Marr got wind of a peculiar singer and lyricist, reclusively stuck in his bedroom across town. Ever resourceful, he befriended a guitarist who knew the specter-like Morrissey to secure an introduction.

---

[*] I admit that Roxy Music formed mainly through musicians wanted ads. That doesn't mean I'm wrong about what a waste of time they are.
[†] Keith was cool, Mick a forward-thinking opportunist—the whole Stones' dynamic crystalized in this one encounter. The exact truth of it should never be questioned. If it turned out to be a fabrication—that they actually met in Woolworths looking through Vera Lynn LPs, the whole history of British rock 'n' roll would collapse. Like Paul McCartney going along to Woolton Village Fete and seeing John Lennon perform "Be-Bop-A-Lula" on the back of a truck, it is a grade A certified rock anecdote. The latter, though, while we're on the subject, provides a pretty good example of fans joining bands too. So taken was Macca with the performance that he went and asked Lennon if he could join the band.

He then went marching round to his house to tell Moz they were going to write songs and form a band. After nudging out the poor guitarist middleman, Morrissey and Marr got down to starting the Smiths.*

Forming a band this way often requires a generous helping of amorality. Like psychedelic sixties pop band The Move. As the youngest and most talented members of three of the city's top bands, they used to run into each other at a late-night diner in Birmingham, indulging in a post-gig carbohydrate. There they hatched a plot over pastry products to leave their current bands in the lurch, form a supergroup, run off to London, and make it. It worked. Though it did eventually give the world ELO and Wizzard. So morality sometimes gets its own back.

Hopefully all this shows that finding the right people to be in the band is actually allowed to be a pleasant process, fun even, and is not as impossible a task as it seems.

Who Plays What—The Personality Test

Hopefully you have now used all this information to go out and find the right band members. But you have only just started forming. Next you have to decide what instruments you're going to play. And I'm not just talking to people who have never played in bands before and who don't know how to play anything at all. No, I mean all of you. The final secret to forming a great band is that it's not what you play, it's who plays what.

The history of rock bands provides a wealth of data to show that certain types of people are more suited to playing certain

---

* As a mark of Marr's ambition, his opening line was "This is how Leiber and Stoller met." Leiber and Stoller were the songwriting partnership behind early rock 'n' roll hits like Elvis's "That's All Right." See, using old rock anecdotes as your guide does have a real track record of being a good way to form a band.

instruments than others. Ignore this and frustrated mediocrity beckons. So I have developed a simple but foolproof test to help you work out who should be playing what (*see Fig. 2, pp. 23–27*). After completing this there will be no more instrument envy, and everyone will be able to express themselves to their satisfaction.

It might turn out that you are all already playing the right things, but it could also be harrowing. You may be about to discover that your guitar collection is as good as firewood to you. Though if you are already glumly preparing the kindling, you might be just the right sort of person to play the bass, so pull one out of the fire before it's too late. Don't get too worried if your band needs some changes. Loads of bands have swapped instruments on starting out. Well the Beatles, Nirvana, and Franz Ferdinand at least, but let's be honest, they're all quite good.* Anyway, if you didn't feel like you needed to change anything about your band, why are you reading this book?

About the Test

In real life, personality tests are a great way of making you feel insecure by writing out in huge capital letters everything you already know and hate about yourself, then telling you it's actually true. But as personality is so important in bands, they are also an ideal way to establish your instrument roles. Real personality tests, like the Myers-Briggs test, have to be carried out in secret by learned professionals or by clumsy computer programs over the Internet, but still don't tell you anything useful—i.e., stuff about bands. So what if you're an ISFJ?† That doesn't tell you if you should be the drummer (actually, if you are an ISFJ, try bass).

---

* Paul McCartney switched to bass from guitar and even had a spell on drums and piano in the days before Ringo. Kurt Cobain of Nirvana and Franz Ferdinand's guitarist, Nick McCarthy, also started on drums.
† Introverted Sensing Feeling Judging—a Protector Guardian—that's what I am apparently and it means I buy good birthday presents.

Read the questions posed in the test and write down the letter that most accurately matches your honest response to each one. Your combination of answers will tell you what sort of band member you are and, from this, guide you toward the right instrument.

Not only will this set you on the path to uninhibited self-expression (or inhibited self-expression if you're . . . actually, I'm going to stop the bass player gags now), it will also help you avoid duplication. There are few things more grim to watch than a band of bass players (I lied). Running from glamour and showmanship, they complete their sensible rock songs with a minimum of attention and fuss. Just as bad, and infinitely more tiring, is the band of compulsive show-offs. Rather than multiplying that band's attention-grabbing chutzpah, such assaults of theater send punters scurrying to the bar, grimacing. The built-in egotism of front-people makes these latter bands thankfully rare occurrences.

But the band of bass players is so common that every night, in London alone, there are at least eight hundred performing, rehearsing, or trying to work out why they aren't famous. Remember that timidly forming a pointless band is just as much an act of bandalism as screwing up a great one. Taking notice of the results of this test should spare you from such a fate. But be warned, people might be about to get upset, or even fired. Actually, I feel a bit guilty now. Right, here we go then.

Good luck . . .

Figure 2. The Bandalistic Personality Test

1. Someone is struggling to carry your equipment off stage.
   Do you?
   - a) Clap him on the back, saying, "Thanks so much for everything you're doing for us. I really appreciate it. There's a pint sitting there for you, by the way."
   - b) Not notice. Look straight past him and head for the bar, flirting with a couple of people on the way.
   - c) Help him, and have an informed conversation about the bass response of the PA.
   - d) Stand around and joke about how this poor wretch spends his time lugging your stuff about.

2. A well-known contemporary hit comes on the jukebox. Do you?
   - a) Come up with a witty or caustic alternative lyric.
   - b) Point out that it's not even the best song off the album and anyway you don't rate them.
   - c) Zone out and listen to the interesting drum break before the bridge.
   - d) Not notice it till the second chorus then sing the wrong words off-key and bellow, "TUUUUNNNE!"

3. You're playing a gig, but the audience is talking, laughing, and shouting abusive comments. Do you?
   - a) Throw your entire soul into the songs and ignore it, performing like this is the greatest show you have ever played, winning everyone over, then later make a sober analysis to see if there's anything you can learn from the experience.

b) Jump off stage and smash someone in the front row in the face with whatever instrument is handy.

c) Go red and try to hide in bits of shadow, counting down every second and playing everything a bit quicker to try and get off stage sooner.

d) Piss on the monitors.

4. It's Saturday lunchtime. You are . . .

a) In a café with the manager making a list of all the people you need to get the single played to and working out novel promotional ideas to get it to them.

b) Sitting in your pants with a hangover shouting abuse at bands on MTV while strumming one guitar chord over and over again absent-mindedly.

c) Taking a stroll into town with your partner.

d) Already on your fourth pint, having been up all night prank-calling your old boss.

5. Sessions are going badly on your first album, nothing's working, and the record company looks like its about to drop you. Do you?

a) Buddy up with the producer, agreeing with all his ideas while secretly telling your management that he's really unprofessional and that you could be doing this in a much cheaper studio.

b) Blame the producer for ruining the vibe you had on the demos and sulk while proposing increasingly elaborate ideas to solve the problems—like hiring loads more gear or recording in a forest in France at midnight.

c) Put down your crossword every so often with a look of supportive concern.

d) Have no idea of the drama because you're playing pool with the roadies and, if you are around, suggest a burping contest.

6. You are at the bar in a venue next to the manager of a huge band. Do you?

    a) Engage her in conversation, somehow casually interest her in your band, and end up exchanging e-mail addresses.

    b) Go barging up and say how shit her band is. Especially compared to yours.

    c) Tell someone you saw her. A couple of days later.

    d) Not see her. Have no idea who she is. Not care anyway and drench her in a pint that you were trying to down while it balanced on the top of someone else's head.

7. You are at another band's gig. Do you?

    a) Stand a little back with a good view, taking mental notes about the best bits of their set, before getting hit on at the bar.

    b) Stand at the back with your arms folded criticizing absolutely everything. Even things that aren't the band's fault. Like how high the ceiling is.

    c) Stand in front of the bassist to get the best view.

    d) Not turn up. Or even get invited.

8. The tour van breaks down at 4:00 a.m. in the middle of nowhere. No one has any money on them, there's no phone reception, and it's pouring with rain. Do you?

a) Convince the tour manager to walk off into the night and look for help while you keep everyone's spirits up with a Beatles singalong.

b) Blame someone for being incompetent, regardless of whether it's their fault, have a hissy fit, and get the assembled entourage to run round trying to find you a drink.

c) Suggest a convincing prognosis for the mechanical failure and try in vain to get someone to listen to you.

d) Get hammered and tell obscene anecdotes.

9. You have somehow landed a support slot with some flavor-of-the-moment arena-fillers. But when you arrive at the venue, you are challenged by security. Do you?

a) Smile and get let through.

b) Scream, "DON'T YOU KNOW WHO I AM?!" and then hiss, "I'm going to remember you. When we headline here, you won't have a job. Okay?"

c) Apologize and wait around for someone to let you in.

d) Offer them drugs as a bribe.

10. A fight breaks out back stage between two members of the band, punches and accusations are flying, a couple of journalists are hanging around and it's only half an hour before you're due onstage for the biggest gig of your career. Do you?

a) Stand in between the warring parties and deliver a poignant but tough speech about the hard times you've been through to get here, leading to a tearful group hug and declarations of undying friendship and reconciliation, while privately marking the card of the person who started it.

b) Take the opportunity to air some of your own grievances about the chap who's getting punched.

c) Stand and look a bit awkward while pretending to read a text message.

d) Turn around, laugh, and make a start on the rider.

Your Answers—The Personality Types

Okay, you completed the test, so check your answers and let's see what you should be playing.

Mainly A's—The Natural Leader

Key features: Some people are born with natural authority. When they tell a story, people hang on every word and explode with mirth at the punchline. They somehow never get interrupted at the crucial moment by someone dropping something, or forget to tell the important part. They are life's designated leaders. It tends to help bands if there is someone in the ranks who has the charisma to capture people's attention. That's part of what bands are supposed to do. These are the unflappable, resourceful people who go through life making things happen. Even when rock 'n' roll fails them, there will be a glittering career ahead somewhere or another. Just look at Tony Blair's career since fronting The Ugly Rumours.

But the Leader can take many forms. Just because they don't freak out and curl up in a fetal ball doesn't mean they all have to be like dull school dorm proctors. Kevin Rowland of Dexy's Midnight Runners used his natural authority to make the band go shoplifting and to steal the master tapes of their first album off the record company in a fearsomely well-drilled heist. While it may be better in the long term if your Leader isn't quite as fond of leading you into a life of petty crime and high-speed police chases, surely better that than being ignored every time you go on stage. Is a criminal record really that much of a sacrifice?

Is this you? Have you answered honestly or just filled in what you think you should have done because you want to keep being the lead singer? Go on—go back to the beginning—you just won't learn will you? Assuming you really are such a leader you can afford to feel pretty safe in the lineup. You aren't going to get kicked out. You might have the odd nervous breakdown, though, and a little bit of a problem with other people having any ideas. In fact, slick and magnanimous as you may be, it hadn't really crossed your mind that other people might have ideas, had it? Or at least not good ones. Not ones that aren't really stupid. Anyway, nothing wrong with a bit of benevolent dictatorship.

What do you play? This is rather obvious. You sing. You might even write the songs too, but you are the figurehead of the band. People sometimes even call you by the band name, so interchangeable are you. Good. You don't want to do all that hard work for nothing.

Mainly B's—The Artist

Key features: The Artist is focused on making truly perfect music. They know they are capable of it because they are so, so good. And they know they are so good because they make sure they are always around people who tell them they are. Which is fine until things start going a bit badly. The price of this talent is a sensitive soul. Or at least a grouchy and spoiled soul. They may be able to wring notes of tremulous beauty from their guitar that leave crowds gasping in tearful awe. But if their amp starts picking up the radio from a local taxi dispatcher it's a different story. Then the guitar's straight through the speakers. And once that tantrum's over, it's time for another one about how their guitar and amp are now broken. "My favorite guitar! Oh fuckin'ell!" and the door slams behind them. As Peter Hook of Joy Division and New Order observed, "There's a fine line between being artistic and a dickhead."

Even the less outwardly temperamental Artist still has at best a slightly tangential relationship with the real world. This is because the real world gets in the way of the important business of life—namely, showing off, daydreaming, and coming up with ideas. Ideas that are equally as likely to be strokes of unparalleled genius as the nonsensical gibberings of the seriously unhinged. Not that anyone is allowed to even imply they're the latter. Then the defenses go up again. Whether that means sulky moods or screaming, the result is the same. Everyone must rush around until things are safely back to normal again. "Normal" in this case meaning that the Artist is safely insulated from workaday hassle. Do not expect such favors in return, though. For someone so sensitive to their own treatment, the Artist has a peculiar blind spot when it comes to the feelings of anyone else at all.

Arrogant, over-opinionated, lazy, and high-strung? Are these all things that have been screamed at you in arguments? Even when these accusations are flying do you secretly think, "So?" Does this sound familiar? Talent comes at a price. You're the one who has given most of your nervous system to the study of musical alchemy. Let the others wait until they are as good as you or have spent as long slaving over the arrangements before they start moaning about your temper. You're not in a band to make friends anyway.

What do you play? You pretty much definitely play something— you might easily be the singer too but you play something. Probably guitar, maybe bass, though there aren't many pedals to fiddle with. Maybe keyboards—and if so you were almost certainly "classically trained." Two lessons playing "Chopsticks" aged seven is another good reason for you to lord your talent over the others.

Mainly C's—The Quiet One
Key features: The unpretentious backbone of the band. Seemingly unmotivated by fame and glory (well apart from deciding

to join a band), they are the everyman. No wild ego trips, no obscure requests on the rider. One of them even provides an ideal name for the type—Black Sabbath bassist Geezer Butler. Geezer—the all round decent, solid guy, and Butler—the honest manservant inhabiting the world of the rich and famous by virtue of an endless capacity to serve uncomplainingly in the shadows. Yet despite individual obscurity, their type is the most universally recognizable in rock. Every band has someone who seems like an ordinary person, skulking in the half-light stage left. Well, maybe not the Velvet Underground, but most anyway.

It might seem like a thankless role. Stories abound of the put upon life of the Quiet One, but there are consolations. This is the rock 'n' roll circus viewed from the best seat in the house. Or as Mat Osman of Suede put it, "Anyone who knows you're the bass player from Suede or the guitarist from Babyshambles likes you. If people hate Suede or hate Babyshambles, they hate the singer. It's a nice way to see rock history but not get your fingers burned." No one's going to come up to the Quiet One in the pub and scream, "Oi! Suede! You're a c**t!"

You may be thinking—I'm not dull—I only answered C's because I'm not a complete asshole. Okay, does this sound fairer? "I'm not especially quiet—it's that the others are incredibly noisy!" John Entwistle from the Who said that—another archetypal quiet one! Come on, face up to it and don't be ashamed. It's one of the best things to be. At least it means you're probably a nice person. Maybe even relatively well balanced. There are other benefits too. Your built-in resistance to making an exhibition of yourself might even be mistaken for taciturn sex appeal—like Gordon Moakes, bassist with Bloc Party. Think of the other advantages—no long nights dredging the bleakest parts of your soul to turn into a catchy chorus.

No interviews. Come up with the odd chord here and there and you might even make a fortune too.

What do you play? Bass. Bass. Bass. Okay sometimes drums or maybe rhythm guitar. But bass—"Hardly a lyrical instrument, the bass tends to attract players of a like disposition. Dogged and even slightly disenchanted, with a robust, no-nonsense approach to performance. Indifferent to applause" (Alan Bennett).

Mainly D's—The Lairy-Mad-for-It-Lunatic

Key features: As I think Shakespeare put it, the Lairy-Mad-for-It-Lunatic is of beer, drugs, and very silly ideas all compact. Silly ideas like throwing empty crates of lager out of moving vehicles, buying a sword and terrorizing the tour bus, or filling the bassist's hotel room with rotten eggs. Will the ceaseless mirth and japery never end? No one has yet managed to explain why the dangerously sociopathic have such a crucial role to play in the twentieth century's greatest artistic legacy. Novelists don't keep a pissed prankster in their house to keep their spirits up with a bit of good old-fashioned irresponsible behavior. But for rock 'n' roll, certainly since Keith Moon first gingerly tugged at a hotel curtain rail, it is almost as essential as being thin, self-obsessed, and below average height. Perhaps they symbolize living the dream—the lawless outsider ideal on which rock 'n' roll secures most of its cool. That's if "living the dream" means a string of antisocial practical jokes from someone fucked up on anything they can lay their hands on.

But before we are too harsh on the band's resident nutter, remember that they fulfill at least one crucial role. Faced with the repetition and waiting around that takes up most of the life of a rock band, it helps to have at least one person in the party whom it's fun to be around. They break up the tedium with a little bit of danger. Mind you, so would discovering the tour bus was full of tigers, and no one would want that. Though John Bonham[*] probably tried it. Just before indiscriminately punching someone.

Equally important is the free publicity for the band. The more dangerous or unhinged the stunt, the more likely you are to get some column inches in the tabloids. Though that really is more for those at the prankster end of the Lunatic spectrum. "Alcoholic drummer of middling indie rock band goes on slightly grim three-day bender around east London," is far less likely to make the front page.

Do you recognize yourself here? Not even a little bit? What about the time you snipped through the wires on the bassist's amp just before you went on stage? When you spiked the singer's smoothie? See—that was fucking hilarious! He was genuinely terrified he was dying! What larks! Why am I being so harsh on you honest rogues? Does everyone in a band have to be some boring fucker with their head wedged up their own ass? No, but not one person who would honestly answer D's to those questions would be reading this book anyway so I can get away with it.

What do you play? Drums. You hit them hard, they're noisy, and they keep both hands and feet occupied, which comes as a great relief to the rest of the band.

Crossbreeds

Not everyone in a band is some kind of freakish gargoyle. There are ordinary people in bands too. Or at least less pronounced types of freakish gargoyle. If your responses were spread across two letters then consult the list below. Anyone whose responses were spread

---

[*] Led Zeppelin's drummer.

evenly across more than two letters, or did not feel adequately represented by any of the answers, is sadly too complicated or grown up to be in a band. Don't moan, you'd hate it—I know the fame and money would be good—and so would making records and everything, but do you have any idea how dull it is most of the time? Seriously, you've had a lucky escape. Maybe go and become a record producer. Or a music journalist.

A's and B's—The Hustler

Key features: The Hustler has the head of the leader and the heart of the artist. The other way round would, after all, be a disaster. They are always on the lookout for opportunities, probably to further their own ends, but for the band that's lucky as that usually coincides with theirs. They know how to talk, are more shaky on listening, and come bounding into the rehearsal room (late) saying things like, "I've got us a gig next Thursday. I bumped into big Dave and he's got us support to (insert cool band of the moment here) for this little party they're doing around someone's flat. It'll be acoustic, so it'll only need two of us but it'll be cool. Be packed. We might need a couple more songs though. Which is cool 'cos I came up with something last night round at Andy's." And before anyone can object he's demonstrating a new song.

This propensity for riding roughshod over other people's feelings can pay great artistic dividends. At one of the first Clash rehearsals guitarist Mick Jones played singer Joe Strummer his new song "I'm so Bored with You" (well, it was the early days of punk). Joe dived in excitedly saying, "Great! Let's write it now— I'm so Bored with the U-S-A." It's a great song and a far better title. Thank goodness he did it. But is it just me that winces a little bit on Mick Jones's behalf? The mitigating factor is that the Hustler is not trying to control anyone, but just believes so enthusiastically in his own ideas that he can't conceive of anyone not sharing them. The other hazard is that, like the Artist, they have so many ideas, and of such differing quality, the band might have to get used to living on constantly shifting terrain. Which is a polite way of saying that sometimes their incessant bullying will make the rest of the band feel like sewing up the Hustler's mouth with guitar strings.

Do you ever shut up? Ever? Or sit down? Or just stop moving? What's wrong with you? If this is you, you'll recognize it. Unless you're actually just an Artist with a really inflated sense of your own social skills. Which, come to think of it, the Artist would probably have. Assuming you are correctly self-diagnosed, you are usually the best thing that can happen to a band. But the combination of your restlessness and their frayed nerves means you can be a disaster if that band wants to stay together for a while. Especially if it's a band with any other A or B personalities in it.

What do you play? Guitar is good—it's flashy and loud. Vocals are possible too. Not much else is likely. You're a bit of a show off, aren't you? Drums if you're tall enough to be seen clearly behind the kit.

A's and C's—The Backseat Driver

Key features: Power is not always obvious. Real power can be virtually invisible. Don't be taken in by those prancing puppets under the spotlights, they're just for show. They're not the ones pulling the strings behind the scenes. There can be a blurred area between the expressions "shrewd operator" and "scheming bastard" and this is often the domain of the Backseat Driver. They don't necessarily care that they don't get spotted in the grocery store's (well, they do a bit—they're as vain and insecure as anyone else in a band) so long as they have money to pay at the checkout. They have the brutal self-belief of the Leader hidden behind an ordinary guy façade.

There is a more benevolent strand to the category too. There are those who just want to be in total and complete control of everything at all times, preferably without anyone noticing or getting suspicious. See, much more benevolent. This category takes in both geniuses and lampooned grotesques. Paul McCartney in particular has had his fair share of being both. If indeed there is a fair share of the latter. It is probably the role in a band that requires the most intelligence to pull off properly. It definitely requires a thick skin.

Organizing a band from within the ranks is never a task that tends to get a lot of thanks. When Dave Balfe joined the Teardrop Explodes, he tried to turn them into a proper band that could play well, had decent songs, and turned up to places on time. The particular thanks he got was singer Julian Cope leaving him stranded at night in the middle of a motorway. Oh, and occasionally receiving the odd beating. Still, despite the fact that the results of his regime were briefly amazing, it does sound a bit like he was asking for it. By the way, no one gives the Backseat Driver any sympathy. Much as you might not feel too sorry for a fat cat falling out of a tree while trying to eat a nest full of birds.

So think back to your last rehearsal. Was there a point when you stopped everyone mid-song and turned to the guitarist, saying, "You're missing that chord in the chorus again! I thought you knew the bit I meant when I said earlier. Do you want me to show you it again?" and suddenly everybody went a bit quiet and subdued?

It's for the good of the band—why do they get so funny about it? Actually do you ever get the feeling the rest of the band socialize without you?

What do you play? Bass, rhythm guitar, maybe keyboards. Like the Quiet One, you play something that will let you stand in the background or not have to concentrate too hard. Unlike them, though, that's because you want to keep an eye on everyone. Also, as it's easy, you don't make many mistakes, so you can maintain a sense of justified superiority over your fumbling underlings. Ha!

A's and D's—The Cool One

Key features: There's a scene in Blur's *Starshaped* tour film, it-self a wonderful document of a band trembling around the rim of implosion, where bassist Alex James and guitarist Graham Coxon are being driven to a soundcheck in a minibus. Graham, despite the full investment of his concentration, is trying in vain to balance a cup of tea on a saucer, hands shaking uncontrol-lably, spilling puddles of it with every jolt in the road. He looks to his side and smiles bitterly. The camera pans over to Alex, staring reflectively out of the window, a full cup and lit cigarette both gracefully hanging from his fingertips with no effort at all. There always seem to be some people who are facing life with the properly updated instruction manual. They are our A's here. The Cool One is this but good-looking and carefree too. Damn them.

This is the person who everyone else in the band secretly wants to be. Not the most talented, not even especially both-ered about being there, just the band's internal totem of cool. They are usually the best looking (not that all-male bands are rampant hothouses of homoeroticism, of course. Actually Status Quo probably isn't. Though all their tour stories do seem to be

about wanking. Let's move on) and probably have outside interests. Don Letts described Paul Simonon as the Clash's "cultural
barometer." What he meant was that he wasn't as sad as the others. They like music but it's not everything. They're more likely
to be found at the bar egging on the Lunatic than up all night
in the studio trying to get the guitars sounding right. They will
have nipped off hours before all that palaver kicked off. While
the Artist has his head wedged against the speakers, they are at
a very cool party the others weren't even invited to.

Sometimes you're a bit embarrassed by the rest of the band. All
they ever do is talk about the fucking band. It's sad. You joined because it's a laugh. It's fun. When it gets all serious and stressful, why
bother doing it? It doesn't matter *that* much. If you really are the
Cool One you are of course very unlikely to be reading a book that
examines and even celebrates the power rituals and mind games of
bands. Though you might be skimming through bits if it's sitting on
the table. Just to look cool.

What do you play? Anything easy—but then you're never going
to make anything look difficult. More likely on bass or even singing
than grimacing your way through an absurdly complicated guitar
solo you spent hours figuring out. Easy drums or single-note keyboard could suit you pretty well too, though. You'd probably even
look good playing a ukulele.

B's and C's—The Moody One

Key features: Quiet doesn't just mean affable and self-effacing.
It can take in moody, difficult, and even downright aggressive.
These are the grumblers for whom nothing is ever quite right.
They might not shout the odds at every turn but they make
sure their presence is felt with an array of sarcastic comments,

awkward silences, and surly frowns. They are masters of the passive aggressive mood. Like the Quiet One, they have their feet firmly on the ground, but in their case it is because they have nailed their shoes there to make a point. Caustic, cantankerous, utterly resistant to bullshit, and constantly on the brink of muttering, "I told you so."

They wage a constant low-key war against undue enthusiasm, anything that could be mistaken for pretentious bollocks and, somewhat ironically, the showy behavioral problems of other band members.* But this is why they are so important in a band. When the studio clock is ticking and a confused argument has developed about what the guitar should do in the bridge they can be relied upon to start playing another riff at increasing volume until they are obliterating everything with background cacophony. Everyone turns round to locate the source of the din. The Moody One responsible looks up witheringly and says, "Oh sorry. Are we ready to play the song then?"

You know what you're like. Moody Ones rarely fail to recognize the trait in themselves. Though the more self-deceiving probably like to use euphemisms like honest or straight talking rather than ill-tempered or intolerant. You get to have the good bits of being the Quiet One but occasionally get people to listen to you too. There isn't all that much to say about the Moody Ones. Which is fitting as you aren't fond of idle chatter. You like to let the music do the talking. Provided the music doesn't try to say something fucking stupid.

---

* For a perfect example of a Moody One cutting a Backseat Driver down to size, see Paul McCartney and George Harrison's famous whispered argument in the Beatles' *Let It Be* film, culminating in George wearily sniping, "I'll play anything you want me to play . . . or I won't play at all if you don't want me to."

You can be found in most positions on stage. Unlike the Quiet Ones, their moody cousins do not necessarily see themselves as only befitting a lifetime in the shadows. But even if you're at the front of the stage there won't be too much showing off. Just a good solid performance. The high quality end of workmanlike. The Who even had one for a lead singer. Roger Daltrey's no-nonsense approach to problem solving was typified by an argument with Pete Townshend over using cumbersome synthesizer backings in their stage show. He settled it by knocking the guitarist out with a single punch. A brutally simple example of no-frills task management.

B's and D's—The Self-Destructive Genius

Key features: One part unholy arrogance, one part guaranteed collision course with oblivion. The Self-Destructive Genius has the unpragmatic talent of the Artist, a taste for intoxication, and is terribly easily led too. In all the possible permutations and paths your career might follow, there is not a single one where this person does not go spectacularly off the rails. In this they are like the intense and cerebral cousin of the Lunatic. Driven in much the same way to flaunt the normal rules of social conduct, they are motivated not by simple hedonism so much as by the dark demons coiling ever tighter around their soul. The result is often the same though—an out of control person in their early twenties running naked down a hotel corridor, screaming, followed by a stream of giggling sycophants nudging them further toward rehab or the abyss. By the age of twenty-eight they will either be dead, have stopped washing and started shouting at traffic, or cleaned up, gotten fat, and transformed into a stiflingly devoted parent.

They will usually start sweet and good-natured if a little excitable. But it won't be long before the rest of the band are having to frisk them for drugs before children's TV appearances or discovering they have disappeared to France for a bit. The Tortured Artist might even start out as a Lunatic or an Artist before falling over the edge. At the beginning, though, they will definitely be good fun and could well be responsible for writing the band's songs. In which case you're all really in trouble. The prognosis is not always bad. The Rolling Stones have an almost unrivaled 50 percent record for keeping Tortured Geniuses alive. Mind you, if Keith Richards was really as out of control as he would like us to believe Mick would have tried to fire him years ago. Either that or just kept him alive enough to maintain the brand and churn out riffs . . . oh . . .

If you got mainly B's and D's you might be feeling a bit alarmed now. Ask yourself these questions—can you imagine yourself in the adult world? Do you get frustrated when people don't understand your musical ideas? Is that because you say things like "The verse doesn't sound spotty enough"? Still looking bad? Maybe now you're really excited about how rock 'n' roll the future looks in this particular crystal ball. Then you're definitely in trouble. If not, consider going straightedge, or at least employing someone to follow you around and keep an eye on you. If you've got a Backseat Driver in the band they'll probably be more than happy to do that for you anyway. Until you try to push them out of the door of an airliner and have to be restrained by cabin crew. Alternatively they might just decide it's safest to fire you now.

What do you play? It depends whether you're more B or D. More D and you're probably just a drummer having a nervous breakdown. More B and you are almost certainly singer and guitarist or maybe singer and bassist.

C's and D's—The Enthusiastic Amateur

Key features: What kind of a boring world would it be if everyone was really good at stuff? Meritocracy is all fine and dandy in theory but in a world where everyone pursues their goals efficiently, in the right field, and to the best of their ability, very few funny things would happen. People wouldn't get things disastrously wrong. During *Live 8*, bickering old men Pink Floyd reminded us all of the importance of the enthusiastic amateur when an excitable Nick Mason came flailing in on the drums about a week early on "Time." Amid skyscraping egos and intense feuding, rock 'n' roll always has a seat warm for well-intentioned incompetence.

"The very best of British rock 'n' roll comes from amateurs with attitude," Phil May of sixties also-rans the Pretty Things reminds us. Our Enthusiastic Amateur is that member of the band who looks like he's concentrating too hard, and whose brother probably owns the van. The concept of Enthusiastic Amateurism has a proud lineage in British rock history. It has been the British band world's backbone since Lonnie Donegan sent the under-entertained children of the fifties wild by playing jaunty versions of Leadbelly songs. Skiffle was born and with it the roots of almost every single British rock band of the sixties and early seventies. The next pivotal point was punk in the mid- to late seventies. In the eighties, the appearance of cheap synths and four-track recorders opened the door again to untrained pretenders, and successive guitar revivals in the nineties and 2000s allowed it to happen all over again. And again.

But Enthusiastic Amateurs are not just there as a symbolic link to music history. They serve as useful musical whipping boys. Nothing makes you feel more like a genius than someone much worse than you. On top of that they're a bit of fun too. Like a four pint Lunatic, and far less dangerous.

Will anyone admit to this one or are you even now hastily rewriting your answers to make yourself look like a Quiet One. Forget it. Be proud to be in this category. You are a very useful person to have in a rock band: friendly, gregarious and probably with a wonderful sense of humor. If you'd wanted to be one of the other ones, surely you'd have bothered to practice more. Enjoy your role. Though your chances of not being canned at some point are admittedly negligible.

You'll take a game stab at playing anything. Best to stick to instruments where there's less competition, though. How about drums? You don't really have to know about notes and things then.

The Results

In an ideal world, your answers will have confirmed that you're all already perfectly suited to playing your chosen instrument. Wonderful. You have formed the right band. Let that inner glow of satisfaction erase all your previous self-doubt, freeing up more time for writing good songs instead of staring blankly into space on the bus thinking you might be screwing your life up. Go on, off to chapter 2 with you, you don't need all this next stuff.

For those of you with more troubling results, it's time to face some brutal facts. Like free market economics, a laissez-faire approach to band politics only creates inequality, jealousy, and inefficiency. You can't just leave it and hope for the best. You need to take some corrective action. First, make sure of the accuracy of the test results by filling in the questions again, this time for each other. It might just be that you were lying about yourselves and are playing the right instruments after all. If not, it's time to swap instruments.

Consult your list of available choices from the character-type sections above and fight it out/argue/meekly accept your fate until you are all playing something. Pick up/sit behind/stand near your new instruments and try playing a song. Not one of yours—a cover of something that you all know and like but isn't too difficult. This might sound a bit rough on the novice drummers, but they'll still have some fun. I've yet to meet anyone who didn't get a deep visceral thrill from thrashing about noisily behind a drum kit. Okay it sounds a bit crappy. Barely listenable even. But I bet that was more exciting than normal. If you practice a bit you'll be amazing.

Oh, it still sounded rubbish, you hated every second of it, and the singer's sitting on the floor crying? All right swap round to your second choice instruments and try again.

Still not right? Have a look at the following troubleshooting charts (*see* Figs. 3–7, *pp.* 45–49). Answer them honestly and they should eliminate any further problems.

Figures 3-7. Troubleshooting Charts

We still need someone to be the guitarist/bassist/drummer/keyboard player/singer/second kazooist . . .

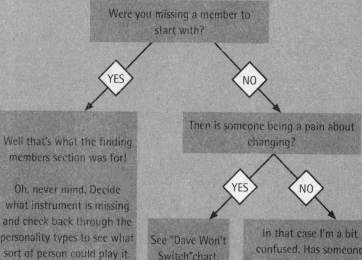

Were you missing a member to start with?

YES

Well that's what the finding members section was for!

Oh, never mind. Decide what instrument is missing and check back through the personality types to see what sort of person could play it.

Then sit down together and think of your coolest friend who fits the bill and get them down to the rehearsal room. It doesn't matter if they can play anything. If necessary, lie and tell them it's a party/bar/private screening of an obscure foreign art house movie, then grab them when they arrive and lock the door.

NO

Then is someone being a pain about changing?

YES

See "Dave Won't Switch" chart.

NO

In that case I'm a bit confused. Has someone just slipped out the room?

Have a look in the toilets or at the studio reception or something. Or maybe give them a ring.

Are you sure they knew it was today? They'll turn up somewhere.

Figure 3

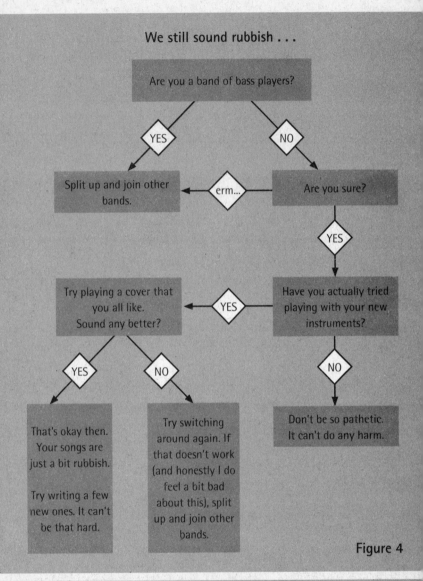

We still sound rubbish . . .

Are you a band of bass players?

YES → Split up and join other bands.

NO → Are you sure? **erm...** → Split up and join other bands.

YES → Have you actually tried playing with your new instruments?

NO → Don't be so pathetic. It can't do any harm.

YES → Try playing a cover that you all like. Sound any better?

YES → That's okay then. Your songs are just a bit rubbish.

Try writing a few new ones. It can't be that hard.

NO → Try switching around again. If that doesn't work (and honestly I do feel a bit bad about this), split up and join other bands.

Figure 4

We actually are a band of bass players . . .

Split up and join other bands.

Figure 4a

It's my band, I don't want to be the fucking drummer . . .

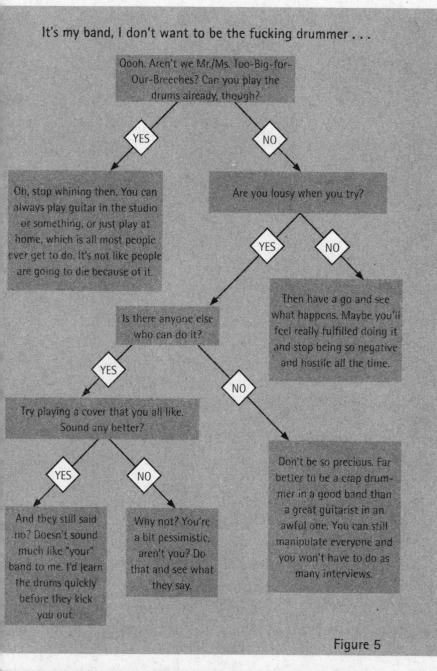

Oooh. Aren't we Mr./Ms. Too-Big-for-Our-Breeches? Can you play the drums already, though?

YES — Oh, stop whining then. You can always play guitar in the studio or something, or just play at home, which is all most people ever get to do. It's not like people are going to die because of it.

NO — Are you lousy when you try?

YES — Is there anyone else who can do it?

NO — Then have a go and see what happens. Maybe you'll feel really fulfilled doing it and stop being so negative and hostile all the time.

YES — Try playing a cover that you all like. Sound any better?

NO — Don't be so precious. Far better to be a crap drummer in a good band than a great guitarist in an awful one. You can still manipulate everyone and you won't have to do as many interviews.

YES — And they still said no? Doesn't sound much like "your" band to me. I'd learn the drums quickly before they kick you out.

NO — Why not? You're a bit pessimistic, aren't you? Do that and see what they say.

Figure 5

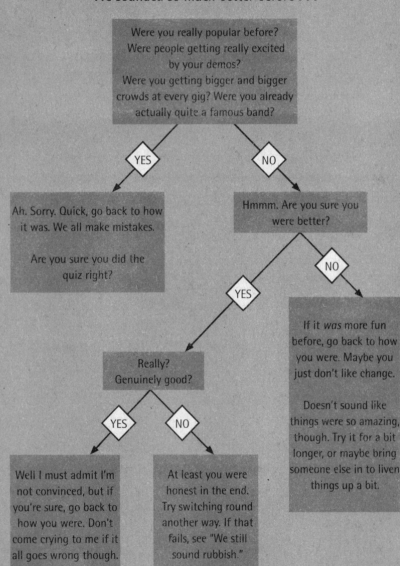

Figure 6

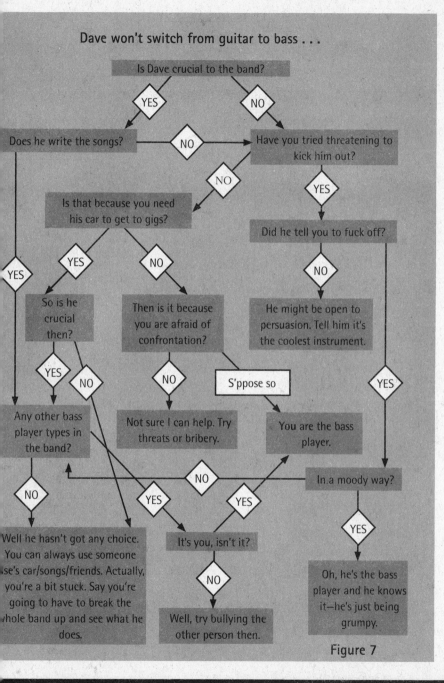

Figure 7

So What Have We Learned?

- If you've counted the carpet tiles on the practice room floor, you're in the wrong band.
- Asking the person next to you on the bus to form a band is always a better idea than consulting the ads in guitar shops. Even if that person is sitting in a puddle.
- How you spend your Saturday mornings will tell you what instrument you should be playing.
- Unless the guitarist also writes the songs or owns the van, they might have to play bass.

GETTING IT TOGETHER

Having followed chapter 1 you should now have all the right people playing the right instruments. By the sheer spontaneous glory of your personalities uniting, wondrous music, exploding with endless possibilities, will rush out of you faster than you can play it.

It can happen. When Jack White's various bands ran aground, he got his wife Meg to bash along with him on the drums so at least he had a rhythm section to play with. It sounded so good that the White Stripes emerged instantly. And, with a bit of lateral association to Meg's favorite swirly red and white peppermint sweets, with an image too. They were almost fully formed from the start.

And that's the final stage of forming—becoming fully formed. Great bands are special because they have an identity. They mean something. Their music, their image, and their attitude all combine to make them so much more than a bunch of people playing tunes together. That's the difference between great bands and terrible ones. It's what makes people want to bankrupt themselves to get every single one of your B-sides, or to catch the odd glimpse of you through rows of tall people at your shows, even to try and dress like you.

But if it doesn't fall into place for you as effortlessly as it did for the White Stripes, it doesn't mean you're doomed forever to be a formless band of bass players. It just means you need to do a bit of work. If fortune's lightning bolt doesn't come crashing through your ceiling unannounced, you may have to cover yourself in aluminum foil, rush out into the rain, and climb up a big tree. Metaphorically. If you have come this far and formed the right band, the answers will be there somewhere. The point of this chapter is to tell you how to find them and unlock your inner greatness. And quite often it involves gratuitously stealing the solutions from famous bands whenever trouble appears.

Getting to Know Each Other

It's unavoidable, the first step is to get to know each other. You can't have a unifying band identity if you've never bothered to find out the bass player's surname. This could either prove excruciatingly awkward or a riotous rollercoaster of zany pranks, but it can't be put off. People like bands because they secretly want to be in the gang. This means you have to actually be a gang. If you're always trying to avoid giving each other eye contact, that's going to be a bit difficult. Which is why most supergroups are terrible.

Apart from helping you forge a band identity, there are practical reasons for going through this. You need to lose your social inhibitions. If you can't tell each other an idea is shit, there will be lots of shit floating about in your songs. And if you have to keep looking up, spoiling the moment, and tentatively affirming, "Oooh, that sounds great, doesn't it?" at every decent drum fill you won't get very far either.

I'm English, so the word I'm about to use makes me want to burn out my tongue and throw the ashes off a bridge. But, in short, you need to "bond." There I've said it. That means that if you don't already know each other, you're going to have to contrive a way of doing so. If you're already old friends or siblings you can skip straight through this bit. But if you're relative strangers, you need a way to break the ice.

The Red Hot Chili Peppers are actually quite good at this. Every time they recruited yet another member in the eighties and nineties to replace one who'd either died, joined another band, or gone a bit funny and run off in the middle of a big tour, the new lineup all went on holiday together. They probably went swimming together or played some sport, which I'm not going to recommend, though if you like that sort of thing I won't stand in your way.*

Based on their policy, here is a less hearty suggestion for clearing the embarrassing bonding hurdle.

A Weekend Away
Arrange to meet in a decent bar near a big railway station on a Friday evening with whatever belongings you deem appropriate for two days away from home. You could then just go through each other's bags. Whatever you have chosen to bring will probably tell you everything you need to know. But assuming you want to retain some privacy, and have a bit more fun, instead get on a train to another part of the country and have an in-joke and anecdote-packed weekend adventure together. You can go wherever you want and do whatever you want. Give yourselves the length of a drink or two to make a plan.

---

* When guitarist John Frusciante first joined they also made him strip naked in front of them. This is probably taking the idea of bonding a bit too far.

If there are two things that force people to learn to get on, they're mutual necessity and poverty. So the only rules are that you have to stay together and return to the same spot together forty-eight hours later, and do the whole thing for as little cash as you can (get the Moody One to specify the budget).

The trip will reveal the majority of your bad habits and tell you whether you can face being in each other's company with nothing specific to do for hours on end. This is how the majority of a successful band's life is spent, so it's good to be prepared. On top of that you will also get a decent working knowledge of each other's mood swings.

When you arrive back at the pub on the Sunday, get out some pens and paper and fill in the answers to the Bandalistic Bonding Questionnaire (*see Fig. 8, p. 55*). Give each band member the same number of blank questionnaires as there are people in your band (i.e,. four band members = four questionnaires each). Take the first one and fill in the answers about the person sitting to your left.

There will probably be a lot of resistance to this idea, but A personality types (the Natural Leaders, Hustlers, and Backseat Drivers from the Personality Test in chapter 1) must use their powers of persuasion to make sure it gets done:

Figure 8. The Bandalistic Bonding Questionnaire

Full name:_____

Given age: _____

Probable real age: _____

Working mental age: _____

Level of personal hygiene (out of ten): _____

Worst habit:_____

_____

Funniest/stupidest/most memorable thing they have said in the last forty-eight hours:_____

_____

_____

Probable ambition aged seven: _____

_____

What they will be doing when they're forty:_____

_____

_____

_____

Draw a
cartoon
of them
(optional):

Fold over the paper and give it to the person you wrote about. DO NOT be tempted to peek at this stage. Repeat the exercise with the person second on your left (then third, fourth, etc. with each pass). You might need extra paper if people have a lot to get off their chest. Keep doing it until each person has a complete set of questionnaires filled in by their comrades. Now, and only now, you can gingerly unfold them and see what everyone else thinks of you. Read them out loud and applaud the most amusing or painfully accurate descriptions.

I refuse to be held responsible for any mental scarring that may occur. Stop whining, you'll have to toughen up some time. The world's a horrible place full of vindictive people trying to use you, steal from you, and shit all over your dreams. There are far worse things to deal with than insulting cartoons.

One final warning—while you're away, avoid talking specifically about any of your songs. Conversations like that, away from your instruments, are always a really bad idea.

Right. Fuck off and bond and don't come back to me until you at least know how to pounce on each other's weak spots.

Rehearsing

With the tasteless stuff out of the way, you can finally get back to your instruments. You shouldn't be on this chapter unless something really exciting happened when you first played together. But now you have to turn that excitement into music. This is the hard bit. Most bands never even reach the status of musically average. But then a lot of bands form with all the wrong people for all the wrong reasons, before finding themselves pushing thirty and back living with their parents with all their joy in life destroyed. You are not these bands. You will not bandalize in the rehearsal room.

Finding the right way to rehearse, and to work out songs, is the crucial part. If you find the right method it will bring the best out of you and take your band to new and dizzying heights. The right method means somewhere you are comfortable being spontaneous but with a bit of pressure to stop you slipping into the habit of pissing about for days on end. If you don't find the right method you'll never feel like you've gelled properly, and what should have been great will slip away before you down the U-bend of fortune.

So, you are looking for something that:
- Forces you to play together (lots)
- Gives you a place to play in
- Gives you a reason to exist
- Is fun (or at least exciting)

The first two are obvious enough, but ignoring the last two is easily done and will definitely make your band pointless?

If you can find a novel or peculiar way of doing all this, it will also give you some much needed mystique and make your band story far more interesting than just—met at school, rehearsed a bit, and played a few gigs. The fact that Def Leppard used to rehearse in an old spoon factory is at least *something* to say about them. Those poor people who spend their lives writing about new bands always sigh when they see the same old dull stories on your press handouts. In fact it makes them far more likely to go and have a nice bit of dinner rather than bothering turning up to watch you play. I'm told.

First Things to Consider
When looking for a way to rehearse, there are a couple of important questions to answer. Firstly, do you want to live together? Or perhaps more realistically, is it possible? There are advantages and

disadvantages to the Monkees-like ideal of the band messing about in a playhouse. It means you can play together whenever you like without needing to keep checking the clock. But it can also sap all of your momentum if rehearsing quickly degenerates into whole days lost watching daytime TV, playing PlayStation, or just sitting about gossiping.

You can leave your stuff set up all the time, but that too can make it harder to actually get down to work. No one wants to be the one who goes and switches their amp on, like a school teacher telling you all to get down to work. But you will probably need one of you to take that role. If you can keep up a sense of forward motion, it can be a really good way to let things develop at their own pace and experiment with ideas without feeling you're wasting valuable time.

Secondly, remember that no band is an island. Whatever type of music you want to make, you presumably hope that at least some people will like it too—whether that's a stadium full of lukewarm fans who will dump you and move on to the next group in a couple of years, or a rabid fanbase of about thirty who have all formed bands in your honor. So when you're rehearsing and working on songs, it helps to find some way of getting them in front of people outside the band to gauge the reaction.

How to Do It

The type of band you want to be should tell you the sort of things to try. A residency as a dance band at a seaside holiday camp was, for example, an ideal way for Manfred Mann to start playing together but would have been less suitable for . . . And You Will Know Us by the Trail of Dead. But how do you decide what sort of band you want to be? How do you divide up bands? By genre? No. Any band would prefer to play nothing than have their music shoveled into a genre. Luckily there is a simpler method.

The Heart-Head Horseshoe

Having trawled through piles of music biographies and carefully noted how each band got it together, I have devised a system to help you find the right rehearsal plan for yours. In general, bands can be placed quite easily on a line between the extremes of heart and head. Heart bands play music that emerges unmolested from the soul, and even sometimes the loins, in its purest and rawest form. Whereas at the other end of the spectrum, Head bands play music driven by the brain, in which every note has a deliberate and considered intention. Heart bands make you dance, Head bands make you think. And all bands fit somewhere between the two extremes. More than that, they actually cluster around a few points on the line.

The line itself is best drawn as a horseshoe because bands at the opposite ends sometimes have more in common than you might expect. Status Quo (Heart) and the Cocteau Twins (Head), for example, both look terrible and don't care, have cultish, loyal fanbases, and an obsession with playing one very specific sound (*see Fig. 9, p. 60*).

Finding Your Spot

So how do you decide where your band fits on the line? Firstly, you need to get together and come up with a list of your collective top ten bands. Don't sit and think about it, just play each other all your favorite records, especially the ones you want to sound like.

After about twelve hours, when you're probably collapsing from lack of sleep or proper food, see which ones you can agree on. Then find the category that fits the majority of them most closely, at least in the period, of their career you like best.

Once you've found your category, follow the links to the suggested rehearsal methods.

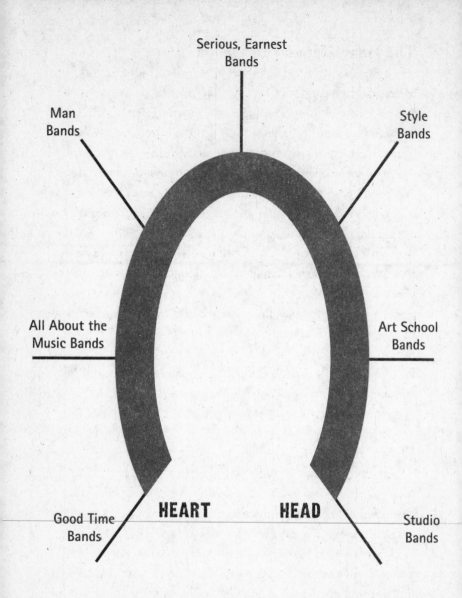

Figure 9. The Heart-Head Horseshoe

The Band Types

1. Good Time Bands

Key features: These are bands that just have a laugh and play for kicks. Music purely for the sake of fun or entertainment with no hidden agendas or dubious philosophies. There is only one serious intention—not thinking about anything much. I am largely writing these bands out of your plan. Not because of any snobbery(-ish), just because no such band could ever be the greatest band of all time.

If you are sure you are one of these, and you've somehow slipped through the net, go to **Playing Live** *(see p. 66)*. Or if that doesn't suit you, you could always try **Covers Bands** *(see p. 79)* or **Garage Bands** *(see p. 71)*.

2. All About the Music Bands

Key features: It could be elaborately technical or hauntingly raw and sparse, absurdly guitary metal or winsome folksy songwriterly softness. But these are bands that don't care if they're cool, they just care about the music. They don't even care if they remain forever cult and niche. They just want to make music that comes out the way their hearts tell them it should. No doubt they would also tell you, if pushed, that they'd prefer to be just be a few people's favorite band, than liked a little bit by everyone, etc.

If this is you, there are lots of different methods you could look at. For a bit of pure organic musicality, try **Getting Away from It All** *(see p. 68)*, or the even cozier **Garage Bands** *(see p. 71)*. If you're desperate to play in front of people, look at **Playing Live** *(see p. 66)*. And if records are more your thing go straight to **The Studio** *(see p. 77)*. As a final resort there's always the more spartan option of **Rehearsal Rooms** *(see p. 73)*.

3. Man Bands

Key features: It's straight-forward, heads-down, and no nonsense. And though there might sometimes be the odd whiff of a concept floating about, that is comfortably overpowered by the stench of armpits, beat-up vans, and old sneakers. They don't care how they look, as long as they don't look like twats. They come in many flavors, but the prevailing taste is usually good ol' rock 'n' roll. Man Bands don't have to be men. Arguably an all-female band like the Donnas is also a Man Band. It is just a state of mind. There's room for the odd bit of instrumental wizardry, even a thoughtful lyric. Just as long as it isn't too flashy and intellectual.

Man Bands too have a lot of choices. Most obviously **Rehearsal Rooms** *(see p. 73)* and **Playing Live** *(p. 66)* are suitably free of pretentiousness. **Playhouse/Squat Rock** *(see p. 70)* might be fun too, though I'd hate to imagine what state the bathroom would end up in. **Garage Bands** *(see p. 71)* is also eminently suitable, especially if you're younger. While **Cover Bands** *(see p. 79)* is always an option if you have your hearts set on paying your dues. Even **Getting Away from It All** *(see p. 68)* worked for Kasabian.

4. Serious Earnest Bands

Key features: With the next step along the line, there comes a slackening of suspicion toward the mind. It's still largely about playing proper music in a proper way, but if they like they can also wear dark clothes, sing about depressing things, and name-check bands that play difficult music too. They're even allowed to quite like books and films. Or sometimes hijack the odd interview to make a point about something outside the world of rock 'n' roll. As long as they're serious and earnest about that too. And don't go on about it in songs too much. They are allowed to look cool, even a little daring, and even flirt with a little bit of camp and humor.

For some gritty edge and bohemian chic, the best start is probably **Playhouse/Squat Rock** *(see p. 70)*, or **Getting Away from It All** *(see p. 68)* for a bit of rock history heritage. Though your natural tendencies might be to aim straight for **Rehearsal Rooms** *(see p. 73)*, the most interesting route for you could also be **The Studio***(see p. 77)*.

5. Style Bands

Key features: It could be a Man Band dressed in frilly shirts, or an Art School Band that wants to write proper pop songs, but between them sit those glitzy, sheeny bands that borrow a bit of everything from everywhere. They are happy to be over the top, musically and visually, as long as they cut a dash while they're doing it. Humor is allowed, high fashion is allowed, even a bit of studio experimentation. They aim for an ideal balance—like perfect dinner companions—well dressed enough to get into the restaurant, suave enough to order the right wine, and good company without being too opinionated or geeky.

Bands of this sort do well by heading straight for **The Studio** *(see p. 77)*, as, historically, it's tended to suit them. If that's too hard, either **Playhouse/Squat Rock** *(see p. 70)*, or **Getting Away from It All** *(see p. 68)*are good for building up suitable mystique. You might even be tempted by **Soundtrack Bands** *(see p. 75)*, though that could seem a bit earnest.

6. Message Bands

Key features: These are bands with an idea. Bands with something to say. They want to provoke a response or push an agenda. They want the band to mean something. Something no doubt very specific. They are serious and committed, though there's still a sliver of heart to keep them accessible and direct. They're clever and they assume the audience is too. Frowning in photos is virtually compulsory. Smoking contemplatively while wearing shades is strongly encouraged. They are allowed to look rock 'n' roll, as long as the look is chosen because it means something. They are allowed a sense of humor too, so long as that's knowing, sharp, and dry rather than cheeky.

Brimming with focused energy as you are, this is the main type of band that can get something from **Rehearsal Rooms** *(see p. 73)*. Though you might be more comfortable with **Playhouse/Squat Rock** *(see p. 68)*. **Garage Bands** *(see p. 71)* could be a bit too domestic, but it's good if you're broke. While if you just want to get out in front of people and shout at them, **Playing Live** *(see p. 66)* is best.

7. Art School Bands

Key features: They are on a mission to shock. To be noticed. To be extreme. To wake up the audience from their vain and lazy love of ordinary, uncomplicated pop music. There is still something new and daring to be found from a couple of guitars and some drums and they are not going to cease their experiments until they find it. They can be very serious or very, very silly indeed but would not be either without a forcefully argued, if often willfully obscure, reason. They might know about cinema, or fashion, or proper grown-up art. They might even just be experts in electronics and effects pedals but they will take their specialist knowledge and use it to go to new, ridiculous or even deeply uncomfortable places and make you think.

The key for Art School bands is making sure it isn't too dull. You are probably already doing **Playhouse/Squat Rock** *(see p. 70)*, but if not, or if you're a little more refined, **Soundtrack Bands** *(see p. 75)* is definitely worth considering. Depending on your musical aims, either **The Studio** *(see p. 77)* or **Playing Live** *(see p. 66)*, or a combination of both, could work for you too. Even a very arch version of **Cover Bands** *(see p. 79)* might be a good start.

8. Studio Bands

Whether their music is soft, twinkly, and womblike or abrasive, dark, and rambling, it comes straight from the imagination. They are perfectionists, afraid that if the bass drum doesn't come out sounding exactly the way it does in their heads, the whole point of their existence will be ruined. They look terrible from working themselves to death in dark, dingy recording studios, but their record sleeves look perfect. For them, music is not frivolous entertainment, but the most meaningful thing on the planet. Ironically, the music they then make is often, to many ears, so controlled that it sounds little more than "nice." But to those who appreciate it, it is like eavesdropping on heaven.

You really need to head straight for **The Studio** *(see p. 77)* or **Garage Bands** *(see p. 71)*. Though if you want some time or inspiration first, and especially if you have slightly disciplinarian tendencies, either **Soundtrack Bands** *(see p. 75)* or **Getting Away from It All** *(see p. 68)* could work.

The Rehearsal Methods

Playing Live

This is the true, organic, rootsy, rock 'n' roll classic. Find a venue where they are prepared to put on slightly wretched bands that haven't quite worked out what they're doing yet and just play in front of people a lot until you have. You can use all the adrenaline of a real audience actually watching you to make yourselves learn to be entertaining.

The most famous example is probably the Beatles, with their residencies in Hamburg between 1960 and 1962. Here they played punishing ten-hour shows every night to fighting sailors, art school dropouts, and strippers taking smoke breaks. As the burly venue manager bellowed, "Mach shau!" they responded with all that head wobbling and cooing that would go on to redefine the twentieth century. It doesn't matter that they got deported a couple of times, had to survive on cornflakes and beer, and sleep under flags, or that they bought some very silly leather trousers. Such things all help to build the myth.

Then there's Led Zeppelin who formed, as the New Yardbirds, to fulfilll a tour that had been booked for the old-very-split-up-and-by-then-just-Jimmy-Page-and-whoever-he-could-find Yardbirds. Not only did they have to learn to play together on stage, they had to do it in front of people who had bought tickets to see a different band, albeit one with the same guitarist and a few of the same songs. How grateful they must have been for the expression "Let's just jam a blues in E."

If you are not the remnants of a more famous band, then it can help if you can get gigs supporting other bands you know, especially ones who are more popular than you and can fill venues. Jack White took that further, playing in the White Stripes as a support act to other Detroit bands he also played in, like 2 Star Tabernacle and the Hentchmen.

Many bands will need no encouragement to get out on stage. For certain types of band, especially Man Bands, paying your dues in rubbish little venues is an inherent part of forming a band. Iron Maiden, to pick just one example, spent years building up a following in pubs around east London till their breakthrough demo got them noticed.

Feedback:

Obviously enough, if you're playing in front of people all of the time, feedback is readily available in its most immediate forms— like cheering and having bottles thrown at you.

Pros:

1. You get to see what bits of your music real people like, rather than just sitting in rehearsal rooms trying to guess.
2. You learn to be comfortable on stage.
3. You have to be entertaining.
4. You get to build a loyal audience quickly.

Cons

1. It suits the rollicking good time band more than the fragile and finely crafted one.
2. It's exhausting.

Getting Away from It All

Go and find yourself a dilapidated old barn in some suitably remote bit of countryside (if there are any left that haven't been converted into luxurious dream homes for burned out stockbrokers). There, unhindered by the vain distractions of modern life and enriched by the wholesome earthy scent of manure and chickens, you can work up your pure musical magic.

A lot of the blame for this pastoral idyll can be laid at the cowboy-booted feet of the Band. Exhausted by eight years of hard livin' and rock 'n' rollin' on the road (including backing Bob Dylan on his infamous first electric tour), they made their way to the peace and tranquillity of upstate New York, away from the clamor of aggrieved folkies shouting "Judas," to plan their next move. Accompanied by an equally frazzled Dylan, they threw themselves into healthy pursuits like choppin' wood and writin' songs. When their first album emerged, it not only gave the world country rock, but also a taste for growing beards, dressing rustic, and holing up in the ass-end of nowhere to write great albums. Neckerchiefs, granddad shirts, and down-home acoustic strumming sprouted across the globe as the formula was endlessly replicated.*

But you can enjoy the country retreat method even if you aren't so set on making pastoral music. Though they occasionally veered that way later, Supergrass's first performances, when they were still noisy, adrenaline-fueled purveyors of power-pop punk, took place in front of a field full of cows in the meadow next to bassist Mickey

---

* Its nadir was surely reached with Balls—a bunch of Brummies, including Trevor Burton, former member of the Move, getting addled in a farmhouse for eighteen months paid for by "leader" Denny Laine. No wonder joining Wings, the most derided band in history besides the Style Council, and willingly signing up to a life in the shadow of Paul McCartney seemed such an attractive proposition to him after that. Ronnie Lane of the Small Faces/Faces also bankrupted himself in the name of the neckerchief with his "Passing Show"—a cripplingly expensive tour around English villages, featuring his band Slim Chance playing as part of a circus show. Unlike Balls though, Slim Chance had some amazing songs.

Quinn's house. Their early demos and first album too were recorded at the Sawmills Studios in Cornwall, well known for being accessible only on a boat or via a long walk down a disused railway line. As already mentioned, sampling stomp-rockers Kasabian also started their musical journey in a deserted farmhouse.

Getting away from it all can also mean more than acres of lush, green countryside. The briefly popular Thrills took a far more glamorous approach. They left their native Dublin behind and followed the trail of their U.S. West Coast musical influences to a beach hut near San Diego, where they lived together for a summer, writing the songs on their first album.

Feedback:

It's tricky to get much feedback from people if you've deliberately decided to hide yourself away from the rest of the world. You have to rely on the fact that when you come back into contact with humanity again, it will be with the purest and most perfect distillation of your musical vision. Or at least with a couple of decent tunes. If you record demos as you go, at least you can send them to people. Though if you can only be reached by paddling halfway out to sea at low tide, they might not bother coming to tell you it's sounding awful. The Internet is quite a boon for the band that wants to be away from everything but still able to communicate with reality when they need to.

Pro:
1. Freedom, endless time, beautiful views, and fresh air.

Con:
1. The high chance of being driven out in a dawn raid by a mob of marauding locals brandishing shot guns after yet another all night jam.

The Playhouse/Squat

If you are a band with one eye on myth, and a taste for all things
grimy, edgy, arty, or cheap, get a house together and make it your
twenty-four-hour rehearsal space and even occasional venue. For a
bit of extra credibility, try taking possession of the place via illicit
means. If all you're doing is playing in a band all day, the squat-rock
approach is also ideal for your nonexistent accommodation budget.

This was very popular in the days of punk when, in London at
least, squattable accommodation was far easier to find. The Clash
did it. Even Scritti Politti did it. In fact, pretty much every London
punk band but the Jam did it.* The most celebrated modern example is the Libertines. Pete and Carl set up home in the suitably
chaotic and debauched "Albion Rooms." There they lived out their
urch-rock fantasies with constant parties, questionable hygiene, and
plenty of spontaneous gigs. With it they developed a myth, a lot of
hangers-on, the odd troublesome personal habit, and of course their
punk-skiffle DIY sound.

Around the same time, those clean-cut clotheshorses Franz Ferdinand did it in far more style. They found a derelict industrial unit,
secured some free electricity, named the place "the Chateau" and
set up camp in their very own rock 'n' roll Bauhaus. They played
shows there too, rigging up some old sunbeds they found on another floor of the building to act as stage lights. Until the police
finally located the source of the noise and came and forcibly shut
them down. Even then they were undeterred, finding a new set of
premises and again calling them the Chateau. If you're going to do
it this way, it seems you really have to name your house.

---

* They stayed living with their parents around Woking in Surrey.

Feedback:

If you let people in to see you play, this method can combine the time and freedom of rehearsing and living together with the instant response of playing gigs. Though as the people turning up to see you will be friends coming round for a party, they might prove to be less brutally honest than your ordinary gig-going punter. Still, in the early stages of a band's development, sometimes it's better if people aren't *too* honest—just a little bit honest. Not enough to make you feel worthless and want to give up. If you record there too you can send your demos out and get some reaction that way.

Pro:

1. You are free to play all day and probably free from paying any rent too.

Cons:

1. The temptation for the constant party to overtake the music. It's hard to rehearse if sixteen people you've never met before are sleeping on top of your guitars.
2. It's a little bit illegal.
3. You are likely to become a magnet for all local dealers, weirdos, and angry local residents societies.

The Garage Band

When means are limited, playing in the garage is always a good option. You don't have to live together or do anything as scary as squatting. You just need one member of the band with access to a room you can go to and make noise at most times of the day. It's particularly useful if you're too young or broke to have left home yet, or at the other end of the scale, if at least one of you is a grown up and has a proper house. It also works if you're just a very quiet band that can get away with rehearsing in someone's flat without constant interruptions from neighbors banging on the walls.

So popular was this method in sixties America, that garage bands became a genre, and a cliché, in their own right. Mainly meaning long-haired schoolboys with an obsession for all things guitar based and British Invasion playing raucous approximations of the Kingsmen's "Louie Louie."

But even in the early eighties, metal giants Metallica made their first tentative musical stirrings in the garage of drummer Lars Ulrich's house. While later still, in the nineties, lo-fi originators Pavement showed impressive efficiency, not to mention frugality, by rehearsing and recording their whole first album, *Slanted & Enchanted* in the space of a week, also in their drummer's garage. Likewise, Pavement's modern heirs the Spinto Band spent most of their teenage years mucking about and recording hundreds of albums on a four track in the basement den/studio they constructed in one of their parents' houses.

It has also worked for distinctly more famous and hi-fi bands. In the sixties, despite being a supergroup (at least one member had been pronounced a God in graffiti anyway),* Cream moved their early rehearsals from a church hall to drummer Ginger Baker's house in the distinctly ordinary north London suburb of Neasden. Not exactly showy, or especially practical for a band noted for playing at stadium volumes, but certainly cheap. It always seems to be the drummer's house that gets used. Playing the noisiest instrument, they are probably already the ones with the most forgiving neighbors.

---

* Eric Clapton—around 1965 the graffito "Clapton is God" was supposedly seen around London.

Feedback:

Aside from one of the band's mums coming in to tell you to shut up, it can be hard to get an idea of what the rest of the world might think of you if you don't take your music beyond the front door. Obviously, finding some way to record it helps, or just playing gigs too.

Pros:
1.   You can watch telly while you play.
2.   It's cheap.
3.   You don't have to commit to living together

Cons:
1.   Someone might need to park their car in your studio.
2.   You need tolerant neighbors.
3.   It can get a bit cozy and aimless.

Rehearsal Rooms

The most obvious first choice for fledgling bands looking for somewhere to play is to head down to the nearest cheap rehearsal room. You can make loads of noise and can use the drums and amps provided, which is helpful if age or finance limit you to getting about by public transport. There are of course big flashy rehearsal rooms too for the better heeled, though most new bands aren't in a position to enjoy such luxury. But while they're helpful for getting songs together before gigs, with the strip lights on and the time measured out in three-hour chunks, they are not all that conducive to coming up with ideas. Especially not when you have to spend the first hour of your session moving everything around after the last band and trying to stop the battered air conditioning unit from hazardously leaking water all over the PA.

There aren't very many bands that go straight from the budget rehearsal room to fame and glory. To be blunt, only bands with the vaguest notions of why they exist, recruited entirely from musicians wanted ads, tend to find themselves in these places. And they are usually doomed:

"Same time next week?"

"Actually, no, I can't do that one because it's my girlfriend's birthday and I've also realized that this is a pointless waste of my time."

"Ah . . . the week after?"

"Yeah, all right . . ."

Here I would love to leap in with six world-conquering, art-changing rock behemoths who all first conjured up their magic in dead midweek slots at Noize Rehearsals. But there aren't any. The closest is the Clash, whose manager Bernie Rhodes basically locked them into his Camden "Rehearsal Rehearsals" studio till they learned to be good. They were there for full days every day and even stopping to eat was seen as traitorous to the cause.[*] Paul Simonon was banished to another room to learn how to play the bass properly and Rhodes himself appeared frequently to inspect the troops and no doubt tell them their songs were all crap.

Feedback:

It's not that cheap rehearsal spaces are useless in themselves. Most bands end up in one at some point. You just have to remember that they are only a room, and therefore only fulfill one of the

---

[*] "Are you here for a goal or are you just eating a cucumber sandwich?" as Rhodes asked first drummer Terry Chimes.

requirements for working out how to play properly together. If you're also playing a lot of gigs or recording they have their uses. But without some extra source of motivation, the bands using them tend to slip rapidly into mediocrity and collapse.

Pros:
1. A great way to hang around in the dodgiest parts of town.
2. They're cheap.
3. You don't need to own a drum kit or any amplifiers.

Con:
1. Virtually everything else.

Soundtrack Bands

It's all very well writing some songs and playing them a few times, but it's not very original is it? If you're trying to push back the boundaries of sonic experimentation, or even just make music that interests you, that seems a cowardly way of going about it. Instead, why not enjoy a bit of artistic cross-pollination and make music to accompany some suitably challenging or bizarre work of art. You can avoid the verse–chorus–middle eight rut, and with any luck something half decent might come out the other end.

Pink Floyd were a run-of-the-mill pop R&B act until their college tutor/landlord asked them to provide music to accompany some of his light shows. That was all the excuse they needed to wheel out the chugging bass lines, start rubbing Zippo lighters up and down the strings of their guitars, and invent space rock. Relieved of the pressure of being entertaining in their own right, but still getting to perform they found it much easier to experiment. Later, in their next lineup, they also wrote some of the music that ended up on

Dark Side of the Moon by providing an unused soundtrack to the film *Zabriskie Point*.[*]

Mercury Rev had an eerily similar start. They provided music for a college tutor's films. Worryingly, if you are thinking of following in these bands' footsteps, their first singers (Syd Barrett and David Baker) both went a bit funny and ran off not long afterward, leaving the rest of the band to get far more famous without them by making one great record then endlessly repeating the formula.[†] It's also far cooler with both bands to pretend you like the earliest stuff best.

Not that providing background music inherently leads to nervous breakdowns. That hasn't happened to Guillemots yet, whose two founding members, Fyfe Dangerfield and Aristazabal Hawkes, first worked together to provide a soundtrack to a promotional video for the architect of a model village in Cheltenham. It's probably not worth waiting for that exact same opportunity to come up. But strange projects can be a good place to start turning yourselves into a band.

Feedback:

It's easy to get some reaction to what you're doing too. If you're providing music for someone else's project and they don't like it then they won't use it. Also it gives people the chance to hear what you do in a different context than just being yet another band that plays gigs and makes records.

---

[*] "Us And Them," if you're interested.

[†] Syd may have played up on stage toward the end, not singing, and covering himself in foaming hair gel, but at least he didn't go to the bar and heckle the rest of the band while they were still on stage as Baker did.

Pros:

1. Gives you to a reason to exist.
2. Gives you a chance to work together without all the creative pressure being on the band.

Con:

1. Your singer might end up going mad and running off.

The Studio

Recording studios are very expensive places. But for some bands, making perfect records is more important than anything else. For the most extreme types, the sole aim of being in a band is to make music aimed directly at an empty slot in their neatly alphabetized record collections. Unless you are already signed, working out your songs amid giant mixing desks and speakers on stands with pretty colored cones is not always feasible. If you're a novice in the studio, it can also be very confusing. But there are still ways in. You can make friends with kindly sound engineers who can get you into studios in the dead slots in the middle of the night. If they like you, they might even help you record too. Or you can set up a home studio and, surrounded by microphones and unusual old bits of equipment covered in winking LEDs, coax yourself into existence through the mixing desk. Computer recording makes that even cheaper and easier.

Queen used studio downtime to record their first album in nighttime sessions spread over more than a year. They also found a producer to help them. And though it sold quite poorly, it got them a record contract and therefore the chance to make more. Around the same time, Roxy Music also went straight into recording, without having to scuff their glittery platform boots on any beer-stained stages. After rehearsing and demo-ing songs for around a year, their management paid for a week of studio time, during which they recorded their first album.

Nile Rodgers of Chic was already a session guitarist when the band got started. He used to take payment for sessions in the form of free studio time so the band could get a chance to work on demos.

Even in the fifties, Buddy Holly and the Crickets got their break from studio owner, producer, and would be showbiz impresario Norman Petty, who encouraged them to come to come to record with him in New Mexico. They recorded there for most of their brief lifespan, and though Petty took an enormous share of their songwriting royalties for the privilege, he helped them to grow and develop rapidly.

Feedback:
The advantage of this method is that you are always making something to listen back to and judge. That makes it far easier to see if you're on the right track with new ideas. Especially if there is someone present from outside the band, like an engineer or producer, who can provide some guidance.

Pros:
1. You know if an idea's good early on.
2. You get used to working in a studio.
3. You can play bits again if you aren't very good yet.
4. You might end up turning into Steely Dan.

Cons:
1. It's either expensive or requires some useful contacts.
2. Unless it's a home studio, you are usually under time pressure.
3. You might end up turning into Steely Dan.

Cover Bands

If you have a band but haven't got any songs yet, there are worse places to start than playing covers. It isn't cool being a wedding band, but even that gives you a chance to learn to play together and perform on stage. People are also far happier to pay you if you're playing songs they know than ones they haven't heard before. If you manage to make enough to live on, you could always combine it with one of the other methods and spend the rest of your time working on your own songs.

When the Beatles played in Hamburg, they were hired as a cover act, as were most of the sixties bands that learned their craft on stage. Even after Lennon and McCartney had moved the goalposts and bands started to think more about writing their own material, the majority still relied on covers for their material. In the UK, that was how bands like the Rolling Stones, the Animals, the Who, Them, and the Kinks all started. Though there are different sorts of cover bands. Those bands were mainly playing very cool and frequently obscure black American R&B and blues songs, not churning out foxtrots in the back of the local working men's club.

Which is closer to how the Jam started. Before punk came whirling around them, cutting their hair (though not bassist Bruce Foxton's) and slimming down their trousers (see previous bracket), they were playing rock 'n' roll standards at an after hours members bar in Surrey. Woking was their Hamburg. It may have taken seeing the Sex Pistols at the Lyceum to make Paul Weller find something to say for himself, but by that time, the band had spent two years playing together. It didn't help their credibility with punk's inner sanctum, but it taught them how to be a proper band.

Mild pop-rockers the Feeling had a similar beginning, though their audience was rather different than the hardened late-night drinkers of seventies Woking. They cut their crowd-pleasing chops in front of the residents of an exclusive French ski resort. Which explains so much. Even the free-form Belgian avant-garde rock band dEUS began life as a cover band. Though in their case it's safe to assume they were more suited to playing Captain Beefheart than a quick blast of "Karma Chameleon."

Feedback:

As a cover band you can usually tell if you're any good because there's always the original version of the song to compare yourself to. Which also means that if you're playing live, the audience will let you know if your versions are convincing. That's if they're listening. If you're not careful, though, some old guy might corner you in the bar and talk to you for hours and hours on end about the bands you're covering.

Pro:

1.   You get to play lots AND earn money.

Con:

1.   You might have to learn all the difficult bits in "Bohemian Rhapsody."

Rehearsal Tips

If you try a method and it doesn't seem to work for you, keep trying my other likely suggestions from your band type list until one does. If all the recommended ones fail then just open the section at random and pick any of the others. If you definitely believe this is the right band, rather than just desperately hope it in the face of all the evidence to the contrary, you will somehow stumble on one that works.

But it might not just be the rehearsal method causing the trouble. There are other common rehearsal problems you are likely to run into. Even if you are churning out stacks of brilliant, original songs, making really good music isn't easy—especially when you have a lot of different personalities all trying to solve the problems and believing their way is best.

On the following pages are five tips for getting the best out of rehearsing. Cut them out and stick them on the practice room wall.

Five Tips for the Perfect Rehearsal

1. Communicate

Lots of potentially great bands founder because they struggle to communicate with one another. As we've already seen, it rarely does bands any harm if they hate one another and channel those feelings into their instruments. But if, instead of coming out in the playing, that anger gets swallowed down and internalized, you end up with lots of unhappy people playing songs they don't like very much and sniping at each other. Having a screaming row to solve the dispute is actually healthier.

Negativity is not always a bad thing, it just depends how it's expressed. Sometimes your B types from chapter 1 (Artists, Moody Ones, and Self-Destructive Geniuses in particular) get a bit carried away and need some firm boundaries. Putting your foot down is far more useful to everyone than grumbling acceptance. It is often repeated that Coldplay's Chris Martin can't even get the rhythm section to play on songs of his they don't like. Drummer Will Champion in particular enjoying an absolute power of veto. Maybe he's still getting back at Chris for that time he got kicked out.

It all comes down to respecting each other's musical judgment. Or at least trying to. A bit. Even if you're the one who writes most of the songs. If you can't possibly take any other member of the band's opinions seriously, you probably shouldn't be in a band with them, or anyone. It will be hell.

2. Be Flexible

Rigidly sticking to the part you normally play on a song is not the same as believing in it or feeling passionately about it. It's just laziness. Hours of painful torment and tantrums can be avoided if you agree between you from the start that your musical ideas are not your living, breathing children. They are just approaches to playing a song. It undermines your good ideas if you cling to your bad ones with equally resolute determination. People will stop listening to you. Or try to practice without you.

You may be right. Your part may be best, but there is only one way of knowing. If you are the one being harangued into re-thinking something, get the others to demonstrate exactly what they want—even playing it on your instrument if necessary. Then play it and make a rough recording (a tape recorder in the room will do). One version of the song with "your" part and the other with "their" part.

Move on to a different song and come back to the recording a couple of days later. If you all genuinely agree on one, go with it. If, more likely, you can't hear a difference between the versions, laugh at each other and play what you want. If there's still division, shelve the song until you can come up with something you all like, while all the time listening out for suitable bits you could steal off other people's records.

Remember too that sometimes things sound wrong just because they are different. Though often, it's because they're crap. To make sure, seek the opinion of someone else (preferably not a blood relative or sexual partner). And don't load the question when you ask them. Just don't spend hours in a theoretical discussion about why an idea does or doesn't work.

3. Don't Play in the Wrong Frame of Mind

Going through the motions is a waste of time. If you don't feel like playing because you're half asleep and want to pass out in front of the telly, or you're feeling sick, or you just really feel like going out instead, don't play. All you will end up doing is depressing yourself and annoying the rest of the band. You'll either be a nuisance, or come up with terrible ideas, or sit vacantly in the corner playing like shit. One big advantage of finding somewhere to rehearse and write that isn't governed by a clock is that you can be more flexible about the way you play, so the odd aborted session doesn't matter as much.

If you don't feel like playing but the rest of the band does, maybe you could play along. But the chances are, something much better will come out of the session if you're not there. Just because you're a band, doesn't mean that you all have to be present when an idea is worked out for it to be good. Dismissing ideas just because they were formulated behind your back is both absolutely pathetic and a great way of destroying the band's sense of unity, trust, and shared purpose.

4. Keep Some Perspective

Every time you get to that bit before the bridge, the bass player keeps fucking it up. It's not even that difficult a part.

This is a really tricky one. There's no easy way around it. You can't say nothing, particularly if it's making the song sound terrible. But saying, "Why are you so fucking stupid—THIS IS HOW IT GOES!" before demonstrating it with a bored expression won't really help. There are a few solutions and all of them are a bit awkward:

- Tell them they need to go away and practice that bit, but try to be friendly and not sound patronizing when you do it.
- Drop it and come up with something else.
- (And very few bands would want to do this one.) Swap instruments for that song.

The first method is best. As long as you're not too much of an asshole about it. But at least credit the hapless victim with some intelligence and let them try to put it right on their own a couple of times before you say anything.

5. Write Lots

If you want to limit the number of the arguments you have, you need to write lots of songs. And preferably find some way of recording them so you can see which ones work best.

The reason for this is fairly obvious. The less precious each individual song is, the more you can feel free to mess about with them and work out your band's sound. Weird songs are good for that. The more unusual the idea the better, as it stops you falling into the rut of playing the same thing on every track. You don't have to play them to anyone outside the rehearsal room, just use them to get more familiar with playing together. That means that when good songs appear it's much easier to get it into shape and sounding good by instinct, rather than having to slave and argue over it. Also, bands sell on quirks. Emphasize your peculiarities and people will remember who you are.

If you listen to the rough recordings among other music too, it can help you avoid another common band trap—writing the kind of songs that no one would actually listen to.

Finding an Image

That's the music sorted, but what does a band that sounds like yours actually look like?

Why Image Is Far More Important Than You Admit

While bands are disproportionately made up of vain show-offs, a surprising number get uncharacteristically reticent when they have to find an image. The majority of bands, and certainly all bad ones, are, it seems, determined to look terrible. In the case of bands at the extremes of the horseshoe, this is easier to understand. Such fripperies as T-shirts and shoes are to them needless impediments in the quest for pure music.

But having an image does not mean you suddenly have to turn into Kiss. A strong image is actually a great way to keep a band focused and together. If you look like a band, you feel like a band. And if you look round the room at the other members and feel like you're part of something—something unique—why would you want to leave?

Even more so in a band built on internal tensions. A unifying image can do a lot to paper over the gaping chasms between you and at least lend you the illusion of fraternal togetherness.

What Makes a Good Image?

Before the C personality types (the Quiet Ones, Moody Ones, and Enthusiastic Amateurs) start fretting about whether someone's going to make them wear bandannas, it is vital to stress that a good image is not the same as an outlandishly tasteless one. That's just as bad as no image at all. Well, nearly. A good image needs to be only three things: unified, recognizable, and suitable.

Unified

The point of a band image is to look like a band. You don't have to wear a uniform and dress identically, but what you do wear needs to share some common aesthetic thread.

Recognizable

If you look like you could be in any contemporary band, your look is probably no good. Julian Cope once said that every artist needs a gimmick. That might offend those of rarefied sensibilities, but he's absolutely right. Name a good one that didn't/doesn't. Cope himself got so fond of his leather trousers, flying jacket, and neckerchief look in the Teardrop Explodes that he wore them solidly (the right word I think) for the duration of an entire coast-to-coast U.S. tour. Which is disgusting, but at least he stuck by his principles. As those *Observer Music Monthly* ads of a few years ago demonstrated with *South Park*–style illustrations of notable bands from Abba to Zappa, the best band images can be re-created in a simple cartoon.

Suitable

Here it's worth referring back to the band categories in the rehearsals section. If the way you look doesn't suit the type of band you're in it's unlikely to work. And if the clothes don't actually suit you or make you look good, burn them and try again. As a quick tip, if you're over twenty-five and the look involves leather trousers, get the matches out.

Where to Look

My pompous pronouncements are all very well, but that doesn't help you know where to look for inspiration. These are usually the most fruitful things to try:

The Coolest Person in the Band

There must be at least one person in the band who looks really good. Or at least a bit better than the rest of you. If you have a Cool One among you, then there definitely is. The quickest and easiest way to find an image is to copy them. Go shopping with them, steal their jeans, follow them round town to see where they get their hair cut if you have to, but just copy them. They won't really mind. People aren't often offended if you tell them they look great. If you do it this way, you have the best chance of looking original and of looking like yourselves.

Other Bands

If you are all just a parade of faceless high street fashion victims, or if the Cool One's a bit short of ideas, you might need to look further afield. Old bands are an especially good source. Even better, old bands whose music you're already copying. The Strokes looked so good that every music loving man was wearing skinny jeans within eighteen months of their appearance, and all they had to do was look at old pictures of Television and Blondie and copy them.

Copying contemporary bands can work too. Best of all was Chic. In 1975, their guitarist Nile Rodgers was stranded in the UK having lost his passport while on tour with another band. A kindly lady showed pity and took him to see Roxy Music. Their high fashion élan and debonair (even chic) demeanor gave him an excellent idea for restyling, rethinking, and renaming his own band when he got back home.

Copying contemporary bands that you also sound like can sometimes work too, but only in the short term, and as a desperate measure. As soon as one great band appears, three hundred more suddenly emerge from their practice rooms, blinking in the unfamiliar light and following like zombies. Look at all those Oasis replicants in the ninties, or the thousands of late eighties hair metal bands, to say nothing of the unkempt, double-fronted urch-rockers hanging from The Libertines' military coattails. That sort of theft doesn't stop your chances of success, in fact it can help in the short term, but once you've hitched a ride on the band wagon, you'll have to be prepared to jump off quickly before you get crushed by other bands scrambling on with you.

Fashion

Not everybody in a band is obsessed with other bands (though it saddens me a little to say it). So if you don't feel like taking your ideas from the world of music, you could always look in the equally unreal world of fashion. It's especially good for haircuts. Fran Healy of Travis borrowed his Fin haircut from the fashionistas of Hoxton and with it filled a million pages of magazine print in the summer of 1999. It says a lot about the moribund band scene of the UK in the late ninties that a squashed, dyed Mohican drew that much attention. Still it was marginally more interesting than the band's music.

If a band cops a look from the ultra fashionable, people tend to assume the band thought of it first. Which is always helpful. Rod Stewart's trademark early seventies feather-cut hair probably came from the grown-out suedehead crops of the more fashionable football fan of the time. But its spread across the football terraces in the years that followed, ironically, owed far more to the popularity of the Faces than to the original source.

As these two examples show, youth cults provide rich pickings. In the UK, at least, mod fashions have spawned several generations of band looks. One of the first, the Who, was famously not mod at all, but the band's early manager Pete Meaden was and saw the commercial potential of getting his band to transform themselves.

Being mods gave them the only decent look of their career and a ready-made audience too.

It's very dangerous if mainstream fashion gets its stylist hands all over a band. A styled look goes against the whole point of a strong band image. Which is not, as people foolishly think, to make bands look good, but to make bands look like gangs. Fashion designers can be a good thing, so long as they're cool and relatively underground. The Sex Pistols looked good in Vivienne Westwood clothes, but then they were already hanging around in her shop before they formed. In fact it was where they formed. Karen O of the Yeah Yeah Yeahs also looks good in the clothes that her designer friend Christian Joy makes for her.

Odd Ones Out—Image Is Power

The Yeah Yeah Yeahs are also notable for being a band that looks good despite not looking totally unified. Which leads us to another crucial part image plays in band togetherness. Image is not just about looking good for the sake of it. Karen and Nick Zinner look fine, but drummer Brian Chase looks like he's just wandered off the street into their photo sessions to ask for directions. And when you look more closely, most bands actually have at least one member who doesn't look right. They are usually in the rhythm section—John Deacon of Queen, Dave Rowntree of Blur, Topper Headon of the Clash, to name a few.* They don't look wrong, or even (dare I say it) ugly, they just look less like core members of the band.

The ultimate example of this is surely Cheap Trick, whose early record sleeves made much of the fact that the band featured two pretty boys with poodle hair, and two guys who were distinctly

---

* All those three were—so is Brian Chase, in fact.

unpretty—thereby producing an image out of the difference between the two camps.

But surely this goes against my earlier point about unity. How can a band look right overall when one or two of the members look a bit wrong? Well this is the other reason why it's so important for bands to have a strong image. As well as making you more memorable to the outside world, what you wear can often be a subtle way of maintaining the band's internal power structures. It's no coincidence, for example, that odd ones out are frequently the last members to join.

At its sometimes sinister end, then, band image can be an internal policeman of hierarchy. Which while it's not very nice, is far less damaging to band stability as a way of solving power conflicts than fistfights or arguments over the music. Sometimes a band not looking identical reminds all the members where they stand. If you need to keep someone in their place, just make sure they're in the crappiest clothes. You can see that in action in the Rolling Stones. The worse Brian Jones* looked in comparison to Mick and Keith, the more his power over the band diminished.

If you think this is fanciful, just look at Dexy's Midnight Runners. In their first lineup, when they were modeling their black woolly hats and leather jackets *On the Waterfront* image, singer Kevin Rowland banned guitarist Al Archer from sporting a red hat because it distracted the audience (from him) too much. Sometimes he even refused to talk to him until the offending headgear was removed. And they were supposedly joint leaders, of a sort. Rowland knew all too well that such knitted flamboyance was undermining his power. In a profound and cerebral world such things probably shouldn't

---

* In his *Rock 'n' Roll Circus* aesthetic nadir, he looked spookily like Wendy Richards in *Are You Being Served?*

matter. But in bands, they do. And keeping the troublesome members dowdy could free your vocal chords up for singing rather than shouting at them.

Seeing What Works

There is only one guaranteed way to see if an image works. That's wearing it and taking photos. Man Bands might think that sounds a bit girly, but it's far less embarrassing than going on stage and being laughed at for looking terrible. The most interested and sartorially trustworthy members of the band (i.e., it's no point sending the drummer) probably need to go out shopping together to try a few things on. You might feel a bit peculiar, but at least you will be doing it all in the noble cause of helping band brilliance and stability.

Finding a Name

To round it all off, you need a name. Most band names are horrible, but you need one. If nothing else, it makes life easier for people who run record shops to file your albums. After a while, however silly they are, band names just become the noise or the set of letters that means your band. Coming up with a good one becomes trickier with each new band that uses up a decent word. As the number of bands in history increases, so the choice for new bands gets smaller. Many might have assumed the barrel was empty when in 2001 four indie psyche-rockers from Leeds actually called themselves the Music.* But still bands think of new things to call themselves. Sometimes even good things.

There aren't any foolproof ways to arrive at a good band name. But there are a few popular places to look. Though, of course, how a band says they came up with their name and how they *actually*

---

* Some might have even thought it about the Band in 1968.

did are not always the same. We stumble again on the fine line between lies and mythology. The Arctic Monkeys claimed in one interview that they got the name from a band the drummer's uncle had been in. It turned out that this was just something they had said to the interviewer because they were bored. And who can blame them? When an interview begins, "So how did you come up with the name?" a poor band's hearts must collectively sink. Still it's lucky they sometimes do ask it or this section would have been far more difficult to research. Using the most widely circulated stories, the names of the bands mentioned in the book so far reveal some obvious potential sources of inspiration:

What You Are

A name that describes what you are or how you want people to see you tends to be a winner. The Small Faces were all faces (the mod slang for someone hip) and were also all short. When Rod Stewart and Ron Wood joined, being less short, they became just the Faces. Cream considered themselves to be the best musicians around at the time. The Band, having had the Honkies turned down by the record label, settled for the way everyone in Woodstock, where they lived, referred to them. The Libertines were would-be libertines. The Beach Boys were cashing in on the surf music boom. Some names are even prophetic. Little did Status Quo know, when they changed their name from the Spectres, just how apt the replacement would prove to be for a band that would become famous for doggedly maintaining the same musical style in defiance of all notions of fashion or taste.

Old Records

If all else fails, you can just look through your record collection. Radiohead took their name from a Talking Heads song, the Rolling

Stones from Muddy Waters, Suede from the Morrissey single "Suede-head," and Pink Floyd from two old blues singers—Floyd Council and Pink Anderson. Apart from the lack of serious effort required, it's also a good way of borrowing some cool from the sort of music you want to be associated with.

Other Band Mythologies

The same goes for borrowing details from the stories of other bands. The Ramones came from Paul McCartney's stage name in an early incarnation of the Beatles when he called himself Paul Ramon (to sound all arty, like). The Beatles themselves, according to one of John Lennon's many versions of the story, were trying to think of a name a bit like the Crickets.[*] The Hollies also used Buddy Holly as an inspiration. Coldplay were especially lazy. They borrowed theirs from another band Chris Martin knew who had decided not to use the name because they found it too depressing.[†]

Things Stolen from Books

William Burroughs has provided a couple—Soft Machine and also Steely Dan, which came from the name of a dildo in *Naked Lunch*. And elsewhere in the world of books, the Velvet Underground took theirs from an erotic novel of the same name, while further down the literary scale, Pulp came from something in a school geography textbook, and the Teardrop Explodes and Belle and Sebastian from cartoons. The type of literature you steal from can also help, as in most of these cases, to tell you something about the band.

---

[*] Or inspired by a dream about a man on a flaming pie saying, "You are The Beatles with an 'a' . . ." Hmmm . . . I know which one I believe . . .

[†] Keane, if one version of the story is to be believed. If so, Tim Rice-Oxley and chums have musically more than called back the loan.

Things Stolen from Films

Oh there are hundreds, but A *Clockwork Orange* is popular. The record shop scene giving us Heaven 17, the milk bar Moloko. Duran Duran comes from *Barbarella*, while My Bloody Valentine and Black Sabbath are, perhaps unsurprisingly, the names of horror movies. Black Rebel Motorcycle Club came from a motorbike gang in *The Wild One*, which also features a gang called the Beetles.

Other Ways

Aside from all these, you could try deliberate misappropriations of football clubs (Saint Etienne or the Kaiser Chiefs), ejaculation (10cc, the Lovin' Spoonful, and probably a few others too), twentieth-century European history (Archduke Franz Ferdinand and the bleaker Joy Division) other people's discarded band names (the Sex Pistols once toyed with being called the Damned), or just moments of suitable inspiration (the Smiths or the Flaming Lips). Or even happy accidents—the Moody Blues were a five-piece band trying to get sponsorship from the local brewery, M&B, that owned the pubs they played in. The brewery insisted, as a condition, they change their name to the dazzlingly imaginative M&B Five. From the M and the B they got the Moody Blues.

As long as you can all largely agree on it and it seems to suggest the right connotations for the band, it will probably do the job. There are more important things to spend your time on than finding an elusive perfect name. Settling for whatever comes to hand is no impediment to greatness. If possible though, it does help if it's easy to remember, easy to spell, easy to look for on search engines, and not too easy to mix up with other bands.

So What Have We Learned?

- You're not a band until you know the bass player's surname.
- Playing your songs over and over for precisely three hours every Tuesday is not rehearsing.
- If you want to live in a squat, you'll have to give it a name.
- Following the keyboard player around town is the easiest way to find an image.

3

THE FIRST ALBUM

It seems to happen so quickly for bands sometimes. While most labor for five grueling years to get their first (ambivalent) mention in the "scene" pages of the local paper, others get wafted casually through into fame's inner sanctum before they've even mastered barre chords.* And because of what you've done so far, you will join these latter chosen ones. By the end of this chapter you'll be touring your first album across the Midwest and maybe even the globe, and having to invest in long-term storage space for all your amassed critical acclaim.

So how will you get there so effortlessly? Well, when you form a fantastic band and play dazzlingly exceptional songs like you've just done, people start talking about you very rapidly—"buzz" as they

---

* The tricky ones you play up the neck of a guitar with a full finger over the strings. I mean this hyperbolically. Even if you are famous, I hope at least one of you can play them. Try a bit of surgical spirit down the length of your first finger. This is starting to sound like John Shuttleworth.

call it. There are very few bands doing something new, original, accessible, and exciting at any given time. Instead there are scores of nearly good bands, and hundreds and thousands of disgracefully unnecessary ones. So the people who make their livings discovering, nurturing, and selling new music tend to be almost indecently grateful when a wonderful new band appears. It wakes them from the stupor that constant exposure to mediocrity otherwise dulls them into. They get all excited and tell all their other industry friends, e-mailing unreleased demos and basking in the type of reflected glory usually reserved for discoverers of new continents.

This only happens when you get absolutely everything right in chapters 1 and 2. As most bands only ever manage a tenth of that, most bands never get noticed. But you have ferociously good songs, a band that sparkles with zealous energy, and an image Topshop will soon be cheaply approximating for the general public. Or have you?

Checking Your MySpace Page

Before you clap yourselves on the back for your breathtaking progress so far, let's just have a little check shall we? You think you look really cool. Your girlfriend even says so. And the FedEx guy when he came to your work. But I know how lazy people in bands are. All you've done is bought a black T-shirt and some sort of fat celtic-looking rings off the market to make yourselves look more dangerous. I know your game.

As you're a band in the modern world, it's safe to assume you have a MySpace page or equivalent (yeah, I hate Rupert Murdoch too . . . blah blah blah . . . but you're a bit stupid if you haven't). Bring it up on screen—it will provide all the evidence needed to work out if you're the future of pop music or just a cowardly band of bass players that has somehow slipped through the net.

If your page has any of the features listed in *Fig. 10*, you're really not trying hard enough. More than 50 percent and you have formed the wrong band. Back to the start with you, before you waste any more time with them. Even if the music's great, you really need to go through the entire image section again.

Only if you can honestly say your page passes the test are you safe to move on to the rest of the chapter.

Figure 10. www.myspace.com/abandofbassplayers

2	**1**	**6**
3	**7**	
	8	
4	**9**	
	10 10 10 10	
	10 10 10 10	
	10 10 10 10	
5		

1: Quote

It's blank.

It shuffles and blushes, muttering something like "Erm . . . we're a band." Wow! Are you that entertaining on stage too?

It is unappealingly complacent—"Getting rid of shit music", "Better than the Beatles", "Fucking awesome."

2: Pictures

You have tried to blur out the bass player.

You are dressed like virtually every other band on earth.

You've taken the plunge with makeup and pouting but are too ugly/old/plain/fat to pull it off.

You have beer guts.

You are pulling a crazy/wacky pose.

You are standing in an alleyway/in front of a graffiti strewn wall trying to look all urban.

You have copied a really famous band photo —but not in a clever self-referential way.

You have copied a really famous band photo in a clever self-referential way.

3: Band Info

You are listed in alphabetical order by surname—so the drummer comes above the singer.

It's blank.

You have made up crazy/wacky surnames.

The majority of the band have sport/male bonding style nicknames, e.g., Phil "Wackers" Clarke—Bass Guitar.

4: Influences/Sounds Like

See Musicians Wanted Ads section from Chapter 1.

Also any of the following:

Sounds like: Nothing on Earth!

[The name of your own band]

The Best Fucking Band on Earth

Seriously, think about it from the point of view of someone who's never heard you—is that actually helpful? Will they warm to your humor or reject your unwelcome invite to be their friend?

5: Comments

They all say "Thanks for the add" and come from other no-hope bands.

There aren't any.

6: Songs

You have put up the three you think are your coolest songs but neglected the only one people actually like.

The download link is grayed out because you're already getting precious about lost publishing royalties, even though no publisher has yet acknowledged you even exist.

7: Gigs

There aren't any.

They are in places near New York City that aren't New York City—like Hoboken or Long Island in pubs that sound suspiciously like they are run by massive brewery chains and have laminated cards on the tables offering $5 meal deals.

8: Blog

It's full of poorly punctuated rants about the manufactured and superficial nature of the music industry.

It's really bleak and depressing—"Sometimes I really wonder what I do this shit for...."

There are only two entries posted two days apart, five months ago—one making angry self-righteous comments about the promoter of a canceled gig, the other a shame-faced apology.

9: Biography

The text contains no paragraph breaks and is as long as it is wide.

It's so stupefyingly dull a read, you can't even remember what it says.

Grimly tenacious factual accuracy overshadows all emotional impact.

It blusters through 400 self-aggrandizing words, which are stretched out like a rack torture trying to tell the story: we met at school, jammed a bit and have played a couple of gigs.

10: Friends

You have the following in your top friends:

Tom

Your individual members' pages

Your boy/girlfriend's pages

Fewer than eight people

Links to those strange porn ladies

Loads of other terrible, no-hope bands

The Music Industry Igloo

For those that made it through, get your suits on, it's time to talk business. Do you want to know what *really* screws bands up? It's their total reluctance to accept that the music industry actually exists or understand the harm and good it can do to them. I'm not going to let you form a perfect band only to throw it all away by having a terrible manager or getting fleeced on your record deal.

After the cozy cocoon of the practice room, heavy with the damp fog of your shared sweat, on first glance, the music industry seems a foul, bewildering place. And on second glance. It's about glance fifteen when you realize there are a lot of good and talented people working in it. People who can get you from rehearsals to record collections without having to break up or apologize into meaninglessness on the way.

It doesn't matter how confidently you stride onto its plains, the music industry is a hostile environment. Its corrosive winds can lash away your brilliance in just a few seconds' exposure. Every time you think about branding, target audiences, demographics, and breakages clauses you are shedding strands of your soul. Bands know this instinctively, so they panic, hide, and most likely get taken in by the first shifty geezer who approaches them and says it will all be fine if they just sign his bit of paper.

But equally you must face an unpalatable fact. A successful band is a business. Not *like* a business. It actually *is* one. And to survive, it must operate as such. But successful businessmen are ruthless and unpleasant and write crap songs. So while acknowledging your status, you must somehow simultaneously hide yourselves from it if you want to do your part of the job properly. It all sounds rather tricky . . .

Luckily, there are lots of people who actually get paid to interact with and work in the music industry, shedding their own souls on your behalf. Usually out of your pocket, granted. You need to construct a shelter inside which you can carry on with the important business—writing songs, looking cool, and getting battered. And while a Kmart value tent is fine for a festival, it is little use in these freezing climes. You must instead construct a music industry igloo (*Fig. 11*).

Figure 11. The Music Industry Igloo

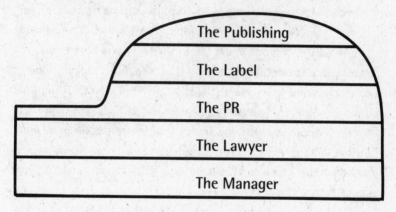

The Publishing

The Label

The PR

The Lawyer

The Manager

To extend the metaphor dangerously close to its elastic limit, if you pick all the wrong people, or just pick anyone who takes you seriously, the layers of the structure won't fit together and fearsome drafts of industry will still whistle through. Take time and, never a nice one for bands, effort, to build the right team around you and you will be able to stay twenty-three till you die (which, of course, might be aged twenty-four if you don't follow chapter 4 properly, but we'll come to that).

So now I will take you through the layers of the igloo and show you what you're looking for.

Layer 1—The Manager

The first step is finding a manager. They are the most crucial part of the structure. If you find the right one, they can freeze their fingers building most of the igloo for you while you sneak down to the lake to catch fish, or whatever metaphorical Inuit bands do with themselves. More usefully you can use your warm hands to write some even better songs.

Finding a manager is not that dissimilar to finding a band member. They need to fit in with the band and to understand how it works and what you're trying to do. It can be anyone from the guitarist's dad's neighbor to some freeloading lackey from a big corporate management company. What the former brings is hunger and instinctive band understanding, what they most likely lack is industry connections and vice versa for the latter. It doesn't matter which you go for as long as they make the required effort to catch up on what they don't know. And this is a trade off which comes up in all your industry dealings. Which you pick depends on what sort of a band you want to be—slick and professional or cozy and familial. Neither is better if it doesn't suit you.

With a manager, though, there is also a personality trade-off. Do you look for someone who complements or contrasts with the band? If they are on your wavelength, they can bully you toward greater heights, come up with ideas with you, and push you to where you think you should be. And hopefully not just sit in bars with you arguing about old records while not actually getting you anywhere near any of the contacts they claim to have. If, though, you have more than enough daft promotional ideas kicking about within the band, you might be better off with a solid administrator, or even a hard-nosed thug, to take care of business. Some bands are better pushed to the sky and others best tethered to the ground.

As with band members, managers come in a limited choice of flavors. Here is an idea of the most popular:

A—The Leader
B—The Visionary

C—The Administrator

D—The Heavy

For consistency, I have given them letters that correspond to the personality types within the band from the quiz in chapter 1, and characterized their traits and all you need to know about them below:

A—The Leader

Who are they? Probably the sort that wear suits, or dress in peculiar sports-casualwear to make themselves look young. Definitely the sort that only deal in benevolent dictatorship. They are right. All the time. They haven't been in the music industry for [insert suitably impressive double figure number of years here] just to be fazed by you lot. They've seen it all before and they know what's best for you. What's more, they have walls lined with gold discs and awards to prove it. Trust them, they will take you far beyond where you want to go. And stop looking at their toupee.

Where you will find them: at big shiny office desks behind buzzer door entry systems and secretaries who you will have stalked with voicemails just to get the chance to get your stinky old Converse near their polished floors.

What to expect: something like a boot camp. No sympathy, no attention beyond a good old threatening showbiz pep-talk, fame, money, success, and a healthy ripping off.

B—The Visionary

Who are they? Like a good TV detective, they are mavericks who don't play by the rules. Full of stupid ideas and genius like their Artist brethren (actually they think they are artists—playing games with pop culture). They will talk in riddles, make grand pronouncements, and always make you feel decidedly uneasy about what might happen next. Brimming with certainty and cynicism they will always be looking for a new angle.

Where you will find them: Hanging around music scenes like vultures. They might even come and find you. You won't like them much when you first meet them. They will seem very peculiar and not blink very much, but their forceful enthusiasm and sinister edge will convince you they can make your band legendary.

What to expect: Being disowned by your grandparents after they make you wear S&M gear on TV, notoriety, and an endless battle against their teeming brains. They will also want to be stars. Bigger stars than you. And will take every opportunity to tell the world that it's them pulling the strings. Not exactly strong on admin, it might be best to accompany them with a more grounded partner. Or slightly more. Much like the Who, when they were still good in the sixties, with managers Kit Lambert and Chris Stamp.

C—The Administrator

Who are they? Talking of grounded types, the C-type manager is also just as solid and dependable as you would expect. Scrupulously fair, unscrupulously dull, and seemingly impervious to the wilder side of rock. When you demand to be winched onstage by a giant crane at the start of every show, they will organize it uncomplainingly but also buy the crane and write it off as a tax deduction. They will, however, suffer quiet apoplexy when things don't go as planned, and those plans will be ferociously detailed. They will get you the greatest record deal in history by exploiting some sort of loophole in the contract wording, but when they come to the studio for the album playback, they will wince and ask you to turn it down.

Where you will find them: In the duller end of the professions, making a fine and wealthy life for themselves but bursting at the seams to involve themselves in the unreachable glamour and excess of show business. A world they will then do everything to shun.

What to expect: A complete ignorance, even bewilderment, at your grand schemes to become the most important band in history and a total absence of anything that might be termed edge or cool. They will barely make up a page in your biography but they will make you (and themselves) very, very rich.

D—The Heavy

Who are they? Dragging on a cigarette, engrossed in conversation with a former boxer in an after-hours drinking club deep in Essex . . . actually no, that's a bit far-fetched, but you know where I'm going. The heavy will terrify you. They will leave you in no doubt that they could do serious harm to you if you crossed them. Actually, they wouldn't, they'd treat you like a daughter, but they like to make people feel that way. They will carry a don't-fuck-with-me attitude around them at all times as if it were a camel hair coat draped over their shoulders.

Where you will find them: You could imagine them just suddenly appearing at gigs or having one of their underlings phone you—even if they don't even manage bands and just run a carpet warehouse. If they are already a reputed band manager, though, you will have to go crawling into their office, no doubt being given some kind of mettle-testing mind-game along the way.

What to expect: Your band will be bonded by collective fear—it will be a band you can't actually leave. Which is obviously quite a blow in the battle against breaking up. The terror will be real though—especially when you become acquainted with their business methods. Expect tales of people being dangled out of windows.*

Of course, in the real world, finding a manager relies more on who-ever happens to be around and, often, who approaches you and asks if they can do the job. The point of this section is to remind you not to be desperate and also to accept the bonuses and drawbacks of whomever you find. If you want them to be something they're not, you'll be perpetually quarreling with them in their shabby of-fices instead of prancing about on stage in front of adoring, obses-sive fans. Knowing what you're looking for is the best way to avoid the manager waking you up in the middle of the night screaming "FORGET YOUR FUCKING DREAMS" and hanging up. Which is terrible for morale.

Layer 2—The Lawyer

I'm not letting you anywhere near recording studios, tour buses, fame, drugs, groupies, glory, or even a management contract, until you've got yourselves a lawyer. You probably think this is dull or irrelevant or deeply un-rock 'n' roll. Or maybe you just don't relish the prospect of spending hundreds of bucks in return for a comatose conversation with a bespectacled man in the Meat-Packing District over cups of weak coffee in corporate branded mugs. I don't blame you for that. But if you need some motivation, go to a bookstore and head for the music biographies (along with the comedy books and DVDs, the only section you know how to find). Pick one at random and look through the index for mention of a court case . . . oh look,

---

* Supposedly a favored method of Don Arden.

there's one . . . oh and another. Other bands through history are just like you—a bit stupid when it comes to thinking about the future unless it concerns fantasizing about taking vengeance on all the people who've stood in their way. But this is the unappetizing lump of broccoli with which you shall earn the arctic roll of success.

The theory is simple. The earlier you find a lawyer, the less time and money you will have to spend engaging with one. Use them from the start for what they are good at—being picky and pedantic and snarling subclauses at everyone who isn't paying their bill. In short, use your lawyer like a guard dog.

And firstly show off their fangs to your new manager. Not that it will make you feel cool, brandishing an attaché case full of densely worded jargon at the Mr./Ms. Big who has finally deigned to give your moth-eaten demos a guarded nod. But the choice is obvious— do that or waste five years of your career and every penny of your royalties fighting a harrowing legal case later.

A deal between publisher and manager squashed the Kinks in the late sixties at a crucial time—losing them momentum, money, and, most ruinously, bassist Pete Quaife, who, exhausted by their litigation, disappeared shortly afterwards to go and get married and live in Denmark. They were never quite the same band again. And how about the Stone Roses? A dispute with their record label, Silvertone, ensured that they released no new material for the first half of the nineties—writing off their prime creative years to courtrooms and cooling their heels. The Beach Boys got a proper stinging too. They challenged their label over not paying bassist and songwriter Brian Wilson his production royalties for expertly manning the mixing desk on their early records. In retaliation, when they left the label, Capitol deleted all these old albums, which contained pretty much all their hits—wiping out a hefty fistful of their income.

A band's creative lifespan does not last forever. I am not going to let you waste a second of it becoming a legal test case. Get off your asses and do some research. Two days on the Internet and the phone investigating suitable entertainment law firms could make more difference than almost anything else in how many great records you get to make. Some of them even let you have a bit of credit if you seem to be going somewhere. It's in their interests when you think about it. For you, it's as good a musical investment as a pre-CBS Fender.* While you're at it you might want to sort out who has the rights to the band name too—a thorny question that's never done screwing up old band members in later life. Then go and do something really rock 'n' roll afterwards to purge yourself of those dirty, sinful feelings of responsibility and wisdom.

Layer 3—The PR

I am assuming you've had to write a resume before. That you've suffered the private, red-faced, sweaty discomfort of trying to sum up your life and your achievements in humiliating bullet points. Nothing reminds you more sharply that, as a human being, you are doomed to experience death alone. If you do not feel profoundly uncomfortable doing that, you are not a human being. You are a sick monster.

While it's slightly easier for a band to write their own press biography, it's marginal. Not only that, you will be bad at it. You will either include too many boring details or slip into some tourette's style invective against all contemporary bands, music, culture, and humanity. Rather than remembering to mention you've done

---

* Instrument geeks prize pre-1965 Fender guitars, before the company was sold to the CBS corporation. Despite most of them never having even seen, let alone touched or played one. Only stockbrokers can actually afford to buy them, sadly. And maybe music business lawyers.

demos with a famous record producer. You will do more harm than good and make yourselves sound like a bunch of clueless twats. Get someone else to do it for you. And that's the easiest bit of a PR person's job. On top of that they know how to get journalists drunk.

If you haven't got a deal yet, you will have to be pretty good to attract a decent independent PR firm. But you've followed chapters 1 and 2, and you are better than good. Even if it's after you've signed to a massive label, independent PRs are always cooler. And, more important, they stop all of your affairs being swallowed up by one company. One company to which you also owe pots of money— never a great political situation to be in.* If that label wants to make back the cash they are going to invest in your first album, they will splash you all over the press till the tills pop out the supermarkets. Great for the ego. Rubbish for the career later on. But we'll come to that in the Press section later.

There are of course great in-house departments at record companies too. You just need to make sure that the people who are telling the world that you are brilliant are as good at their job as you are at yours. Make sure they understand where you want to go and you can blithely let them get on with helping you get there.

Layer 4—The Record Company

I don't care who you sign your deal with. I don't even care if you dismiss record deals as things of the past and sell all your MP3s online from your bedroom. But seeing as the point of this section is getting other people to do as much of the music business for you as possible, I'm going to assume you'll put someone in charge of peddling your ditties to the general public. Even if it's your mom.

---

* Remember, a record company advance is not a gift, it is a loan—you have to earn it all back again. Six gleaming figures of empowerment-paralyzing debt.

And I'm not going to tell you how to get a deal. Sorry. But there isn't any kind of quick fix to that. If you have followed the instructions so far, that won't be anywhere near as hard as it is for most bands. Just aim for labels that sign bands like yours.

The record company won't rip you off too badly now you've got yourselves a fine legal brain involved. They aren't even *that* evil. They just want to make as much money from your records as possible. As do you, come to think of it. Some of the people working there might even genuinely like your band—play the records at home to their friends and everything. Treat them as human beings, and they might return the favor by working extra hard for you—even fighting the odd battle on your behalf. And you need as many people like that on your side as you can get.

You see, contrary to what you might believe, record companies are not staffed by robot warriors of capitalism, marching you deliberately to your demise. Not exclusively. Even the absolutely huge ones have a liberal smattering of nice ordinary people in their twenties and thirties who work in music (and have worked hard to work in music) because they really like it and care about it.

This does not mean that the label will always have your band's best interests at heart, though. Making as much money from your records as possible can often crash head on with what's best for you. Despite having marketed music made by self-contained bands for about fifty years (i.e., about half the lifespan of the record industry), companies who peddle records and deal with bands every working day still have barely the slightest clue how musicians work. They can be forgiven of course. I use a computer every day but I couldn't build one, and scream swear words at mine and hit it with my shoes when it does something I don't like. So it is with record companies and bands.

But by failing to understand the finely balanced and complex series of relationships that make great bands great, or even to acknowledge that bands actually contain complex relationships, record companies consistently repeat the same errors and destroy them. Short of an enlightened job exchange scheme, you must instead take it upon yourselves to make sure this doesn't happen to you.

So here's the rule. Let them do what they like unless it seems to damage anything you built up for the band in chapters 1 and 2. While you're brilliant, they might not feel like doing that. In fact, stay brilliant and you'll have very little trouble with your label at all. And trouble means forced image changes and fiddling about with your lineup. It's the latter you really need to guard against at the start.

Drummers are usually most at risk. Record companies usually try and pick off the weakest members. And that's assuming they're being benignly incompetent and trying to make the band better. They may actually have signed the band just to get at the singer. Then you're all in trouble. But assuming the former, to a record company, what does the drummer actually do? Play the drums, yes . . . and piss away cash on stupid rider demands. You can sort of see their point actually. So if the drummer starts not turning up to places, or getting into trouble with the police, or even just playing badly, you can hardly expect your label to shrug their shoulders and go, "Yeeeaah, but that's just Paul! You know what he's like!" On the balance sheet, you see, Paul looks a bit troubling. Particularly compared to some fifty-year-old session guy who played bongos on the last Pink Floyd tour. Paul costs more, can't play as well, and stinks.

But as we know, Paul is crucial to the band. You can't just swap him—unless you can find someone else just as perfect. And that virtually never happens. So there's no point risking it. Paul may be an irritating, unreliable twat, but in bands, that is no reason whatsoever to kick someone out.

Why? Because THEN THE BAND IS OVER.* You will instantly cease to mean anything. You'll stop making decent records, or even worse won't even get to make one at all. At least if you stand together and they drop the whole band, you are a full band that can look somewhere else. If you got signed by one faceless multinational company and are still good, another one will probably appear to take you off their hands. Or you could even go to a small record company that might actually know something about bands instead.

So keep hold of the band and its identity—that's what you know about. Let them market your music—that's their job. That way, sticking to what you each know best, even your record company can be part of your protective wall against dealing with the miseries of the industry.

Layer 5—The Publishing

Publishing royalties are the money that songwriters make from the use of their songs. An extra wedge of cash for being so clever. There are two big hazards when it comes to bands and music publishing. The first is getting signed to a viciously small royalty rate, so the publishing company makes most of the money from the songs. But again, we have our lawyer to stop that happening.

The second is more damaging. And this time it's your responsibility to solve it before a publisher even gets involved. There are many great bands that have hung their glory on the gargantuan writing

---

* Pedants would step in here and say the Beatles swapped Pete Best for Ringo Starr due to pressure from the record label and it didn't do them any harm. But the pedants would be wrong. All George Martin and Parlophone did was employ a session drummer for recording (pretty standard practice with new bands in the studio in the early sixties—the same happened to the Kinks a couple of years later). It was the band who wanted to change, somewhat against the wishes of their manager Brian Epstein. And they wanted to change because they wanted to be in a band with their friend playing the drums, not someone they didn't really like all that much. That's a far better reason to swap.

talents of one or two of their members. There are far fewer examples of those same unquestionable geniuses going on to make records that are equally good in their later careers with other bands.

In fact, name three:

1. _____

2. _____

3. _____

If this stays blank then perhaps you need to think again about whether they are the only ones responsible for writing the songs. Whether or not you see this as a conclusive argument in favor of royalty democracy, deciding how you are going to divide song credits should be established from the start. I know it's boring and likely to end in an argument, but if you don't do it now, it will be one of the most likely things to break up the band in the future. And by then, real money will be at stake.

Even a band as non-evil and non-money-grabbing as Nirvana nearly came unstuck on that one. Kurt Cobain got very belligerent when Krist Novoselic and Dave Grohl demanded a bigger share. Once *Nevermind* had sold millions, they realized what they were missing out on. They were all somewhat myopic not to have seen it coming, even if they never realiszed how much money was about to roll in. It was basically resolved, but maybe the bad feeling explains why the follow-up, *In Utero*, appeared to be such a deliberate act of commercial suicide (if you pardon the expression).

The Band too went into rapid creative decline the moment they realized that guitarist Robbie Robertson was getting the majority of the publishing credits. If you know their records and how crucial each of their individual contributions are to the songs, particularly Levon Helm's drumming, it's hard not to sympathize with the latter's resentment. U2, though, who divide writing credits equally, have sustained a thirty-year career without even a lineup change. Hmmm . . .

It's not that people in bands are just after the cash. Rather that bands work best when they're a team effort, and if one or two people are far richer than all of the others, that can be hard to sustain. The main songwriter(s) may get resentful if the drummer gets paid for doing nothing while they make themselves sick writing lyrics. In which case, just give the drummer a smaller share. But in a proper band making proper music (i.e., all members contributing to the unique effect), they should still get *something*. If for no other reason, it buys goodwill, reduces division, and keeps everybody interested.

IMPORTANT

You may not turn the page until the publishing split is settled.

Properly.

By the whole of the group.

And witnessed by your lawyer.

Right then, at ease. That's the dull stuff dealt with. This should all stop the industry tearing your band apart. Time to crawl into your igloo and make some music. Your first album, to be precise.

The First Album

With your band all perfectly imperfect and the industry at bay, you move toward your first album. There will be groundbreaking singles and a growing buzz on the way, but your aim is set on this first crucial statement. The record that will infiltrate the brains of millions, or even just diehard thousands, but leave a lasting impression.

That means you have to record it, promote it, and live with it, in vans, cheap hotels, modest tour buses, radio studios, and on rowdy or catatonic international flights—and live with each other—for eighteen months. And you have to do that without irrevocable fallings-out and without embarrassing yourselves or losing you way. It sounds almost impossible. But not for you. Because you will know what's coming. So here is a guide to avoiding bandalism at the next stage—recording, promoting, and touring the first album.

Studio Hell

Whether it's cheap studios and singles or plush sofas, big speakers, and a full album project, the recording studio shimmers into view on the horizon. You have arrived. Quick! E-mail all your friends saying you'd love to meet up for a drink but you can't because you're in Abbey Road a for couple of weeks—yeah, *that* Abbey Road. No not just in a pub, recording in the actual studio and everything. Then rush off to the bathroom and pull a Springsteen pose in the mirror. This is what you've been waiting for.

But rock 'n' roll is littered with the corpses of bands that have stridden confidently across the metaphorical zebra crossing never to return. Even great bands like yours with fine songs and a decent look. Yes, the studio hides dark perils in its dank chambers. When you walk to the bathroom for a bit of peace and quiet after an aborted and revolting take 1,065 of your first A-side it might feel like some of the magic has already started to disappear. In fact, you may find yourself looking at the bathroom window and sizing up the potential for escape.

But it doesn't have to come to that. The hazards of the studio are as avoidable as any others in the band's life.

Demos

And they begin before you've even carted your gear through the doors into wood-paneled nirvana. The ability to demo songs outside the studio is a double-edged sword. In our high-tech modern times, a free evening and a computer are pretty much all you need to make decent-ish recordings. You'd think this might be a great help for a band going into a proper studio for the first time.

But in the wrong hands (and those would be the hands of most people in bands who can be bothered to make elaborate home recordings), a fully realized demo is a guaranteed source of studio tension. The musical equivalent of asking your girl/boyfriend to tell you all about all the other people they have slept with. Only even more aggravating and painful.

For when the demo is brandished about by its creator as the ideal (i.e., only) interpretation of a song, trouble is afoot. The other members of the band feel a bit redundant—only one step up from being your programmed servants. That means they might not be all that inclined (or even allowed) to give their best, uninhibited performances, or contribute their ideas. Which means the recording definitely won't have the same precious "feel" as the demo that you keep blathering on about. It will be being made by people who *feel* hurt and fed up. It also means it won't feel all that much like a band. It will be static and lifeless and without soul. The very things that bands are not supposed to be.

Demos are brilliant for testing arrangement ideas to see if they work, but what matters are the proper recordings. And for a band, those are only good if everyone is playing out of their skins. They are very unlikely to be in the mood if the guitarist is keeping everyone waiting for three hours fiddling with her amp to find the exact, elusive sound of the demo. If you want to avoid the first obvious avoidable source of tension, grit your teeth and leave the demo at home.

Going in too Soon

But of course, like the best things that come out of recording studios, the flipside is just as important. At least our demo-wielding psychopath has an idea of what she wants the record to sound like. Equally as dangerous is the totally clueless band that goes in blithely assuming that the studio itself will suddenly crackle into life and fill them with hundreds of great ideas. In the fabulous liner notes to Ben Folds Five's "Whatever & Ever Amen," Mr. Folds comments that "arrangements were rehearsed or at least discussed," prior to recording. Bands regularly omit this precaution.

If you go to record a song that is only half-written, everyone will have an idea of how to fix it. Even the drummer. Now do you see the problem? Most of your very expensive time will be wasted in trying to tell each other why all your ideas are shit. Which means all members will cling even more tightly to their suggestions. Which means . . . well all the stuff we've already noted in the Rehearsal Tips in chapter 2 as being not great for band morale.

Producers

Which is where the producer comes in. The advantage (and disadvantage) to going into a big proper grown up studio is that you don't tend to get let in without having someone in charge. At least that someone can also take some responsibility for helping you hold the sessions together.

But holding the band together is not their job. Their job is to make a great record on time. When the band needs a peace summit, some producers might take it upon themselves to roll a joint, give an hour's lecture on the reasons behind conflict in the Middle East, and make you all help them rearrange the furniture until the room has the right vibe. Most producers, in fact. And annoyingly, it can get good musical results. If that means the Moody One storms out, it's you and the manager who will have to entice them back. Not the producer. Though if the Moody One plays well and has a nice, recordable amp, said producer will be far more keen to help you.

In theory, at least, the producer is there to get the atmosphere right, get the best out of you, and get you to concentrate on doing a decent job. No doubt eagerly backed up and agreed with by the Backseat Driver (oh, they love studios). Hence picking the right producer is frustratingly essential. Like many bands, you might not think you need one and decide to do it yourselves. But unless you really know what you're doing in a studio—not just with old mics, but with your vision for the project and how arrangements fit together—in fact, unless you're a bit trained in music's technical arts, this isn't advisable.

Sadly, unlike managers, finding the right producer is far too complicated for anything like strict guidelines to be provided about it. Feeling like you want to tie them down to their swivel chair and shoot all the members of their family in front of them has little relation to whether they are the "right" producer. Drunk legend Guy Stevens spent half of the Clash's *London Calling* sessions swinging big metal ladders about, making huge collapsing stacks of plastic chairs, and pouring bottles of wine into the studio piano—all during takes—yet still created the right atmosphere to make that classic album. While Brian Eno, though a collaborator rather than producer on Bowie's three Berlin albums, no doubt infuriated the band with his "oblique strategies" cards—cards he stuck up on the wall with, well, oblique suggestions on how to approach their parts. A producer can do pretty much anything they like as long as it works—and most things are worth a try. Energy or enthusiasm are usually good signs. And, like managers, producers that create a sense of exciting forward motion do a lot to stop band members from feeling like walking out.

For all their importance in the life of a band, picking the right producer is usually just a combination of luck, trying to work with the people who made your favorite records and the pragmatism of using people you can afford. Working with a famous one makes more people pay attention to you, while working with an unknown can make the process more like a mutual and bracing exploration into uncharted sonic lands, and hence, more fun. Though as it's unlikely to be the band itself paying the bill, it is also unlikely to be you who gets the final say in who you work with. Which is a bitch, but still, it's one less choice to worry about. All you can do is strap on your twat detector and hope for the best.

Emergency Remedies—In Praise of the Tantrum

If things are going wrong on in the studio and you have exhausted the Rehearsal Tips from chapter 2, sometimes a good old tantrum is just the thing. Though they must be carefully deployed. The Kinks provide the best example of the judicious use of a hissy fit. They had already recorded two versions of their breakthrough, genre-spawning single, "You Really Got Me" by the time they finally got it right. And with one flop single behind them already, neither producer Shel Talmy, nor their record label, were especially keen to lavish yet more studio time on them. But Ray Davies, singer, guitarist, and never a man of undue modesty, was absolutely convinced that his creation was brilliant. He sulked them into the studio a third time,

firing the band up, and maybe scaring them a bit too, with his zealous enthusiasm. They cut the definitive version in the one take they
were allowed.

It was a gamble. If the version had been crap, the band would
probably have been dropped and split up. But then if they'd settled
on the on the crap version, and it had flopped, the same would have
happened anyway. It was a calculated risk and about the only option
to save the band's career.

Such acts of rash heroism can be just what is needed at times of
studio pressure. But only pull them if you really believe you *know*
how to solve the problems with a song. Otherwise all those grateful
slaps on the back you're imagining will become vicious blows on
the face as you shout the track away to disaster and lose your deal.

Not Breaking Up in the Studio

The best insurance against the studio winning the battle is to be
realistic. Making records is not always easy and you have to learn
how to do it. Led Zeppelin may have recorded their first album in
three days, but they were only ripping off old blues songs, and two of
the members were very experienced session musicians. Some sorts
of music are just harder to record and feel a bit more like pulling
teeth before you get an end product that's as satisfying. Sometimes
it just doesn't work because it was the wrong studio/producer/day.
More often though it's because people panic when it gets difficult.
Recording studios are frustrating places, and if you're not prepared
for that they will frighten you into feelings of inadequacy. Realize
what can go wrong and you'll probably be fine.

Promotion

But making it out of the studio with something worth unleashing
is only part of the story. It's a useless endeavor if people never hear

it. This is why you have built your igloo. That team of people are ready to make you megastars. Or at least well-loved underachievers, depending on your tastes.

But if you dive into promoting the record with nary a care, blindly hoping for the best, you will probably have torn apart the fabric of the band in a bandalistic frenzy even before the first bathroom break on your first low rent tour. You need to throw yourselves at the waiting world. But you don't need to screw up everything you've achieved so far in the process. Keep your head and this should all be quite painless.

The Press

Firstly it's the press. But even as you're applying a light dusting of blusher and pouting for the camera in a modish brick-lined photo studio, you can still undo all your good work by acting like a big tit. How you appear in the press can have a dramatic, if somewhat unwelcome, influence on the lifespan of your band. Here's what you need to look out for:

Hype—Your Name with the Word "Mania" Stuck on the End

Hype is a great destroyer of bands. If you rush on to the world's stage shouting, "WE'RE THE BEST FUCKING BAND ON EARTH!!!" with tastemakers chanting your name from the wings, and then trip over or just mumble an apology into the (metaphorical) microphone, it will all be over. A band that has made a public show of being an embarrassing disappointment will struggle to regain people's interest. Like the then hotly tipped Magazine's only *Top of the Pops* appearance, when singer Howard Devoto stared into the camera looking a bit scared and a great single actually went down the charts as a result. If this happens to you, those journalists who championed you at the start will be so ashamed of themselves that they'll rush to decry you in print at every opportunity, or pretend you don't exist, to make up for their error. And a band that people are determined to hate, however united and bonded its members may be, is finished, because it has no future. Unless it radically reinvents itself.

So remember how the music press survives. It tells people which records to buy and hence sells advertising space to record companies and music lifestyle brands. To do that it has to sell magazines. It does that by finding bands it thinks people will like, getting hype going about them, and hence making people want to read about them and hence buy the magazines. In the best cases, it does it with wit, panache, and style, and by hailing your band as geniuses. But it has no inherent interest in your future. When you are desperately trying to appease the press with a compromised, self-conscious second album, it will discard you and pluck the next band from the eight billion who are waiting to fill your place. Accept its compliments and chastisements and then shrug them off like they were coming from a plump aunt.

Hype is more of a risk to some bands than others. If your band is just being itself—making the sound that this collection of musicians wants to make—hype is far less dangerous. If you are good, there will always be people who want to listen to you and you will need the press less to convince them that that's a good thing to do with their time.

If you are average and just brashly talking yourselves up, on the other hand, you will be on course for the backlash—that moment where the press calls back the loan of its goodwill and sends in the heavies to claim it back. Your faults as a band will be put under exacting scrutiny—far more than if you'd just kept your gob shut. Look at Embrace's Danny McNamara or the Others' Dominic Masters, who harmed their bands' careers by annoying everyone (until Chris Martin resuscitated a humbled Embrace).

Once people have decided you are idiots, they are less inclined to believe in you.

Some bands are even dragged into the spotlight almost by accident. If you appear at the depths of a musical lull, you may find yourselves championed as timely saviors just because you're in the right place at the right moment. That happened to Veruca Salt in the gap that followed grunge, or Terris after the Britpop hangover of 2000. When the next big thing arrives and displaces you, at least you won't be hated, but you will be forgotten, which can be just as bad. So be wary of being pushed too hard too soon just to fill a hole, when you could build your fanbase more slowly and keep it for longer. If you are impatient for success and grab at it too fast, you will lose it again just as quickly because the public will have had less time to grow to love you.

If you walk straight onto the front covers in an unexpected fanfare, do the cool thing and play it down. Claim not to know what the fuss is about—you know you're good but you don't want to be all over magazines and in everyone's face all the time. The Arctic Monkeys model—be your own backlash.

Alternatively, your genius might fall on deaf ears. You might be struggling to even get your gigs reviewed despite believing you're doing everything right. Then it's worth remembering that many successful bands with long careers are always hated by the press. Particularly if their trade is relatively unchallenging mainstream pop/rock. Specialist genres have their press guardians, normal pop music less so. The feeling being that if lots of people will like it anyway, no one needs to defend it. If this is you, you must be aware that your dealings with the press will be a bit nasty. Seek solace in the fact that you will be able to spend on dinner what most of your critics spend on rent in a year. And don't let the weekly batterings divert you from the musical course you want to follow.

But the press is fickle. It has to be able to do its job. Being cruci-
fied for the first couple of years is no barrier to being loved in the
end. Radiohead and U2 were both denounced as dull-minded copy-
ists until they matured into being untouchable heroes. They were
strong enough as bands to stick together and force themselves to
progress. If you have got it right this far, you will be too.

Survive the Savage Scenesters

So how do you get your band through it? It depends what type of
band you are. Some bands need the press more, some bands deal
with the press better. Different bands present different risks. Whichever category you fitted into on the Heart-Head Horseshoe in chapter 2 will tell you the best way to avoid getting washed up on the
newsprint rocks.

Good Time Bands

You will be hated. Or impolitely ignored. Your only mentions will
be in pieces about other bands in sentences that begin, "At least it's
not as bad as . . ." Get used to it and ignore it. Your unpretentious,
antifashion status will be exactly what appeals to most of your fans.
Don't try to go all clever and complex just to make the press like
you. It will fail and your existing fans will desert you, horrified.

All About the Music Bands

If you're earnest and lucky enough you might just get a brief spell
of headline time. But your lack of interest in the more superficial
bits of rock 'n' roll will catch up with you in the end. Once the press
stops wanting to define you (say as part of a new scene, or because
there aren't enough showy bands to talk about that week) they will
lose interest. Even a Phil Spector production credit wasn't enough
to get as much attention for Starsailor's second album as their first.

Your only option is to follow your own hearts. You're not about hype and showbiz anyway, so don't be surprised if hype and showbiz display as much snotty apathy toward you.

Man Bands

You will probably be okay, as long as your music isn't too derivative of bands who were popular a couple of years ago. Then you can expect the knives to be out from the start. Otherwise, your natural bullishness will be your savior. You will stick so rigidly to your love of straightforward rock 'n' roll that you will be more benignly ridiculed than hated. You will never get in-depth critical acclaim, but you really shouldn't be looking for it. Not from a bunch of hipsters. Just try to avoid making fun of other bands too much, unless you're good or funny enough to get away with it.

Serious Earnest Bands

You are in a trickier position. Being cool or credible, or at least being taken seriously, is the backbone of your identity. But journalists love poking fun at bands that take themselves too seriously. Unless your singer is strikingly cool and good-looking, you must expect a few laughs at your expense. Like All About the Music Bands, you have to stick to the kind of music you want to make. If you are sure among yourselves that you're cool/serious/intelligent, other people will believe it too and you can carve out a cult fanbase. If, however, you try to use the oxygen of mainstream popularity to breathe all the life into your brooding mystique, it will all be over in months.

Style Bands

You really need the press. You are part of fashion, part of a moment in time. The secret to your survival is constant (stylish) reinvention.

You need to be hip with every move you make. Either that or you need to grab your one moment of being in the right place at the right time and hope you build enough fans and sell enough records to last beyond it. You have to take the biggest risk with the press. For your band to work, it has to be in vogue. You need to be very strongly bonded as individuals, or be shrewd and cynical operators to survive a backlash in one piece.

Message Bands

You may not need the press to affirm your cool credentials, but you need interviews and exposure to communicate your inspiring wisdom to your devoted fans. You are hijacking the press in order to hammer home your preaching to your legion of followers and hopefully attract new converts with your zeal. As long as your message is entertaining and novel enough, the press will be your friend. They will like filling pages with your pronouncements and selling vast numbers of extra copies of magazines every time you are on the cover, due to the rabid loyalty of your fanbase. When you're not the main feature they will of course take every opportunity to lambast you, but that will only keep your message alive. For you, it all depends on not getting boring. Then you will just be ignored.

Art School Bands

You will tease and play with the press—always appearing well-defined and self-aware. Or at least that's the plan. Always remember that people hate to be manipulated. No, that's not true—people hate to *know* they're being manipulated. Gay Dad came a cropper because they thought they knew how to play the game. That and because they made terrible records. Either way, their speedy rise and fall had much to do with the press's suspicion of their motives. Not that they were an Art School Band—far more a hustling Style Band. Proper Art School Bands in the Sonic Youth mold—those that are more like All About the Music Bands but with a fiercely intellectual agenda—will probably find unconditional love in the press. At least after they've been around for a while. Mainly because journalists will be too scared to admit they're not clever enough to understand them. Just don't tell them that or you'll be hated forever too.

Studio Bands

Highly conceptual Studio Bands often have a journalistic past anyway—like Saint Etienne or, if you count them as a band, the Pet Shop Boys. Or, like Steely Dan, they are just smart and calculating enough to understand this world instinctively. You already speak the language so you don't need a lecture from me. Playing live might scare the life out of you, but talking or posing is what you have spent a lifetime preparing for. Awkward sonic pioneers, though, who love the studio because it is more ordered than the hurly-burly of the real world, should be more on their guard. Your only option is reclusiveness. If all your interviews degenerate into polite conversations about recording techniques, you will be quickly glossed over. Better to refuse to talk. Then no one will ever get to be disappointed by how dull or inept you are compared with your records.

Believing Your Own Press

It's all very well knowing what you need from the press and what it can do to you. But what about when you actually thumb through a magazine and see what it has to say about you? When you stare in shock at your band's name in 10-point black type accompanied by gushing praise or ridicule.

Reading your own reviews is a peculiar experience. Sometimes they hurt a lot. Far more than you would have expected.

For example, take the old review cliché:

> "w is like x doing y to z"

where:

- **w** = your band/song
- **x** = a band or song within the same genre as you
- **y** = a show of the reviewer's glittering verbal brilliance, usually referring to an act of love or of extreme violence
- **z** = a band or song which has some unexpected similarities to you/yours

Bands don't often break up because of bad reviews.* But they can cause real trouble later when you are writing a song and suddenly self-conscious about not wanting to sound like band x or z. When that happens you suddenly stop feeling indestructible and accidentally find yourselves making music not for yourselves but for other people. That is a game you can never win, and a big part of what the outside world does to make bands get worse with time.

You formed your band in the first two chapters because it felt right. And that's the spirit you need to maintain. If it still feels good to you then it probably is good. You can't let reviewers dilute that. But it can be hard to stay so buoyant when you have just read the sentence, "The most frustrating thing about this album is that it's unmitigated shit," about something you've given a year of your life to.

There is no easy solution to this. You just have to remember that good reviews sell records more than bad ones stop them being bought. And that your music is likely to outlast the review. There

---

* Though it was the final straw for two of mine.

aren't any TV programs where celebrities discuss the top ten album reviews they have read but there are quite a few about the albums themselves. Similarly, there are hundreds of examples of classic albums getting pasted in print when they first appeared.

Wearing Sunglasses at Christmas Dinner

And ecstatic press? You might be referred to in print as things like "genius" or "god." Which is quite nice, isn't it? Maybe you secretly agree with them a bit too. I mean you are *quite special*. Actually, yeah, you are a fucking genius. YES. At which point it is very easy to forget all the hard work involved in being a "genius" and start flouncing about saying that songs come to you in visions, or pulling a cracker with your auntie at Christmas dinner while wearing a giant pair of mirrored Polaroids.

Ian McCulloch of Echo and the Bunnymen stopped bothering with soundchecks after a while, as they were so clearly beneath him. Something enflamed by his lionized status in the press at the time. As guitarist Will Sergeant observed, "He was starting to think he was God—but even God has to soundcheck sometimes."

Nothing puts an unnecessary strain on band relationships like one of you suddenly deciding to become a self-important twat. This is often referred to as believing your own press. If you behave like that in private around the band too, they will stop feeling any motivation to work, or even talk, with you. For the rest of the band there is only one sure-fire solution—to tease you mercilessly until you snap out of it and grow up. A few pride mortifying acts of humiliation should stop you talking in that ridiculous mid-Atlantic accent in no time. It's a risk to take with band unity but far less of a risk than being in a band with an idiot.

Selling Out

"What do you mean we've fucking sold out? Don't be so indie! What's wrong with making a bit of cash? It's called the music *business*! Everyone else makes money out of us I don't see why we shouldn't have some."

Cue songs being used in the background of ads for razors and the complete destruction of all artistic credibility. If hype is the risk with the press, selling out is the risk in the rest of your promotional activities.

That said it's worth remembering a couple of practical points before you start branding the bass player a traitor for getting free bass strings in return for being listed among the famous players on the back of the strings packet.

Firstly, in modern times, people are so commercially bulldozed and numb that you can get away with a whole heap of lucrative selling out before you get caught. Sponsored gigs, for example.

Secondly, some fans, those most precious supporters of all things indie, will think you're a sell out if you buy a new pair of sneakers, or play to more than fifty people. Don't worry about them. They are not actually your fans. They are the selfless fans of "new music" who disseminate the word about you so that your real fans get to hear about you. They will move on in days and so will you.

So let's get something straight. Selling out is real. It does exist and doing it is a willful act of bandalism. But what the phrase *means* depends on what sort of band you are to start with. Selling out is not just sticking your songs on commercials or smoothing off your musical rough edges to make yourselves more palatable to a wider audience. Neither of those is inherently wrong. Selling out is becoming something different than what you set out to be in order to make a desperate leap into the big time. If you are shamelessly keen on fame and money from the start then you can afford to be more cavalier about courting dirty cash. It isn't against everything you stand for. Fugazi* doing a Gap ad, on the other hand, would be quite a different proposition.

There are perfectly forgivable reasons why it happens. Record companies and music publishers need to make money. They do that by selling and licensing the rights to as much of your music as possible and offering your services—a slice of your image and cool—to all kinds of companies who could do with leeching a bit of youth credibility. Using you as a great big billboard. Your long term career is of little practical importance to them. Most bands break up or get dropped after only a couple of albums. The more money the record company milks from the first one, the more they recover their initial investment (like the three months in the studio you have already had at their expense). The small percentage of bands that actually do stick together make them far more money than the other ones they bleed dry. But for the record company, taking the risk that every band they sign will make seven platinum selling albums and treating them accordingly would be on the mental side of imprudent.

If they do not pressure you into selling your souls for cash, they are not doing a very good job. But ignore them. As with pressure over band members, a band that gets dropped as a going concern, complete and with identity and reputation intact is always in a better position than one that rips itself apart in guilty confusion after taking up residence in Babylon.

This isn't a political issue. I'm not trying to push a radical anti-capitalist agenda. It's a bad idea because it pisses off the people who like you for the sake of a few months being quite liked by the people who couldn't really give a shit. It alienates the people who subsidize your career (your fans) and dilutes your band identity in the

---

* Ruthlessly self-sufficient and anticommercial hardcore pioneers.

bargain. And if you do that, you will make an awful second album because you won't know who it's for—you? Your old fans? Your new fans? Your bank accounts?

The best advice can be paraphrased from David Bowie—if you think you're gonna make it, you'd better hang on to yourselves. And he should know, just look at what happened to the poor Dame when he tried to sell shares in himself . . .

Touring

With your commercial and critical stock in the ascendant, it's time to get on the road and show the kids some of your crazy rock 'n' roll. And charge them a fortune for the privilege. Yes, it's touring time. You are about to enter an exhausting parallel universe. One where time is measured in itineraries, where place names cease to exist and where days are turned on their heads. You are locked together in enforced intimacy, watching the normal world go by from the corner of a truck stop. A universe of sleep-deprivation, hijinks, misery, waiting about, frayed tempers, wandering into record shops in strange towns and playing the same songs over and over again to the point of meaninglessness. Hurrah!

If before your band was rather like the giddy first flush of romance, now you have moved on to living together, making excuses to avoid sex, and fighting in Ikea.

Touring is of course a different experience for different bands. To some it is the high point of the job—the lifeblood of rock 'n' roll. To others it is only one tiny rung above working in a call center in its dispiriting impact on quality of life and creativity.

One might imagine that this spectrum of feelings would map fairly neatly on to the Heart-Head Horseshoe of band types. But I'm afraid it doesn't. While the touring lifestyle often tends to suit heart bands better (way too much dangerous thinking time for head bands), this is not a reliable way to predict which bands will survive in one piece most easily on the road. In fact it's less about what sort of band you are but how you react, as individuals, to the process. This section is a guide to personal, and hence band, survival—how to protect your mind, your soul, and your body against bandalism on tour.

1—The Mind
Communication
You don't have to spend every passing mile of highway discussing your most intimate feelings and playing trust games. But you do need to find a way to avoid repeatedly getting on each other's nerves, just because you haven't bothered to check how anyone else is feeling.

Oh I'm sure it wasn't like this in the good old days of rock 'n' roll. We've all seen photos of Deep Purple sitting on their big plane looking cross with each other and scared of Ritchie Blackmore. But that was before Spinal Tap and sponsored tours. We live in a very different world now.

If your band is already a seething mass of tensions and loathings, touring will be like putting yourselves under a microscope in the path of the sun. Whatever type of band you are, you will have to learn to speak your minds. Tell each other your feelings. Or, if you are the sort of people who would prefer to internalize everything and risk a stroke rather than actually engage in direct communication (and you are in a band so I'll assume it's this one), at least learn to read the nuances of one another's behavior. If you don't, lots of unnecessary arguments and threatened walkouts will be coming your way.

Particularly if you haven't known each other long. It can be all too easy to misread even the most basic moods—to interpret "I'm down, cheer me up" as "Fuck off I hate you" (or even more disastrously, vice versa). After a couple of weeks of that, the Moody One could be halfway back to the airport, spilling his guts out to a journalist before you even realize he's gone missing. And by then it might be too late for the band.

You might think at this point that I'm living in some touchy-feely ivory tower, that this rubbish is entirely irrelevant to the nature of life on the rock 'n' roll highway. But think about it. If your first album's any good and you're signed to a major or largish label, it's more than likely you'll have to spend eighteen months on and off the road promoting it. First national support tour, festivals, dates abroad, a big tour of your own once single number three has appeared, more international dates trying to break into new markets, and back for the festivals again. That's a long time to be unaware that shouting in the morning makes the bassist want to piss on your breakfast. Some very experienced tour managers have assured me during the course of researching this book (i.e., sitting in pubs) that the one thing above all others that they've seen break up bands is lack of proper communication.

I have heard tales of a very successful contemporary band in which members aren't allowed to go to sleep angry but must air their grievances or forget them. Which seems a pretty good model to copy. Or you could have one area of the bus or allotted time of day where grievances can be raised without reprisal. This is trickier, though. If you call the guitarist a twat, there *will* be reprisals, he will hit you and sulk. Still, at least that gets it out in the open.

A Very Easy Solution
If these methods still seem far too close to direct communication, I have devised one that removes the interaction from functional emotional harmony.

Get yourself down to a Staples and buy the following:
- four packs of different colored Post-it notes for each member of the band
- a Bic pen each
- a piece of letter-sized paper each

Agree between you which emotional condition each of the four colors of Post-it note will represent. For example:

Yellow	=	Do you hate me?
Pink	=	You're being a twat
Blue	=	I'm miserable
Green	=	Leave me alone

Take the sheets of paper and assign one to each member of the band, writing their name at the top. Then stick them within easy reach on the tour bus.

If the keyboard player seems to be ignoring you but is being fine with everyone else, take a yellow sticker, scribble your initials on the back, and stick it to their card. You have communicated, and it was painless. The keyboard player can then either say, "Oh, don't be stupid, I'm just beat," or stick a pink one back on your card. Then you can go and ask what you've done.

Or maybe you want some time to yourself. Then stick a green one on everyone's board. Or just on the drummer's.*

---

* This method was inspired by a touring game the Animals played in the mid-sixties. A strip of two-sided sticky tape was stuck on the tour bus for each band member, with a mouth drawn below and eyes and nose above. Every time they slept with someone on the tour, they had to steal a pubic hair and attach it to their strip. The winner was the person who ended the tour with the biggest "mustache." My version is far more responsible and less objectifying of other human beings, I'm sure you'll agree. Maybe you could stick your Post-it notes onto a face too. Tears for sad things maybe. Sorry, I'm getting carried away . . .

Oh, I know what you're thinking. Ha ha—who do you think we are? Keane??!! No band on earth would do that. Imagine a young Happy Mondays fucking about with Post-it notes. Quite. They broke up messily after degenerating away their talent. If you don't want to break up, you may have to grow up. Far less cool, but also far less of an insult to the poor fuckers who bought your records and hoped you'd make a few more good ones before the feuding and disintegration set in. You might not fancy this method, but you need to work something out. Being able to communicate with each other on a level above the Neanderthal is not a weak pansy's vanity, it is in fact THE ONLY THING THAT WILL KEEP YOUR STUPID BAND TOGETHER.

2—The Soul

Packing Your Bag

Right, taking care of your soul is mainly about packing your bag properly. A sentiment I suspect my grandmother would have agreed with. First step, hygiene. Being smelly on tour is an unnecessary step toward disintegration. No one likes smelly people. Being clean makes you feel human. Forget having enough clothes. You can buy them or go to the Laundromat. All you need to pack are a big stack of underwear and more than one pair of sneakers. Chuck in deodorant and loads of toothpaste and that's hygiene pretty much covered. This is less about packing for comfort and more about packing for sanity. The rest of your suitcase also needs to be assembled with that in mind.

The Portable Sensory Deprivation Tank

You will need time to yourself. It will stop you going mad and falling out with each other. Here then is a guide to the guerrilla creation of personal space:

- **Sunglasses and a portable device for listening to music**—shades and an iPod will buy you more quality you-time than you could possibly imagine. You will also look really cool when you do it, as the endless white lines of the motorway whiz past on the front of the lenses
- **Earplugs**—particularly brilliant for wiping out the dull, distracting, low-level din of buses, aircraft, and other members of the band
- **Your phone**—so that you can text the outside world. Even better if it's one of the fancy ones you can get e-mails on
- **Sleeping tablets, vitamin pills, and shitloads of painkillers**—okay this is the dodgy side of responsible, suggesting you take a bit fat bundle of drugs around with you. But they're all legal and truly essential to your well being and sanity

See—you could almost fit that lot in your pockets. And though doing that might require purchasing a very sturdy belt, just these few items can buy you back your individuality and personal space.

You might also want to chuck in a load of books too if you're that way inclined (and if you are, I like you more). Make sure you pack two piles, though—trash for reading on your own and show off books to intimidate the others with your intellectual might. Try sitting at the back of the bus reading Machiavelli's *The Prince* while chuckling and archly looking around. Though don't do that if you're in some horribly machismo-obsessed band in which a desire to be educated is viewed with hatred and suspicion. Then just getting all the way through *Kerrang!* will make the rest of the band think you're trying to be Melvyn Bragg.

Finally, a very, very carefully hidden credit card might not be a bad idea. Not in the drug paraphernalia sense, you understand, just for emergency secret money.

Burst the Bubble

Unlike every other part of the book so far, being in a perpetual band bubble is not actually such a good idea when you're on tour. Not just because it makes you get on each other's nerves. But because it wastes your spirit of togetherness on bullshit like bickering with each other, when you could have saved it up for working on new songs. If you get too domestic and insular it will be harder to give as much edge in your nightly performances and to feel like a cool and creative band next time you're working on new songs. Instead, stay apart—read the paper, buy new records, and keep remembering the outside world actually exists.

3—The Body

There's a thing Robert Elms does on his radio show in the UK where he asks eminent celebrity guests how they would spend an ideal day off in London. Most of them say visits to the theater and walks on Primrose Hill. Which is all lovely of course. Give me such a fantasy day off, though, and I know all too well how I would spend it. I would most likely get up about midday, try and buy some clothes but not really like any of them, grab a pint, have a second and a bag of crisps, buy a few records half-drunk, talk nonsense to some friends in another pub, decide to go and buy a DVD to go home and watch but get waylaid by a boring gig in a little indie venue, get my dinner from my favorite emergency eatery* about

---

* I won't mention the name. Suffice to say, though, it's a chip shop in north London that also serves beer, stays open most of the night, and sometimes features an Elvis impersonator singing in the restaurant bit.

1:00 a.m. and stagger home, all to the accompaniment of about eighty cigarettes.

Why do I mention this? Because I don't think I'm alone among twenty-somethings on the fringes of the music industry in being compulsively self-indulgent and mildly self-destructive when given a couple of hours to kill. And if your daily routine involves starting work about 5:00 p.m. with a soundcheck, then an hour and half's real work at about 9:30 p.m. with, apart from the odd interview and photo shoot, pretty much nothing else to do but travel, the temptation to get battered is hard to avoid. Especially as it makes the time pass quicker.

Even if this doesn't affect your performance on stage, it's probably not the best regime to settle into on a long tour. Without your mom/partner/another responsible adult on hand to stop you, excess can quickly slide into illness. And illness means "nervous exhaustion" and a "throat infection."

Why is this a problem? Well, when a band member starts suffering from these ailments, gigs get pulled, and they may have already passed a point of no return. You are then rushing toward news stories in the *NME* about your new bassist, the old one having decided to "take a break for a while" by "mutual consent" to recover from "nervous exhaustion." Translation—you're fucked. The bassist has left and you're suddenly not a proper band anymore (although Arctic Monkeys seem to be an exception).

So you have to learn to look after yourself. Unless you're managed by your dad, no one else is going to do it for you.

The Bryan Ferry Self-Diagnosis "Throat Infection" Thermometer

Roxy Music raise their makeup-heavy heads again. Having got in the charts with their first single and got famous before they'd played more than a handful of slightly awkward gigs, Roxy Music must have been daunted by its American tour. It is, after all, a country that likes its musicians to be competent. On its eve, Bryan Ferry announced that he had a throat infection, and their attempted U.S. conquest was postponed. I have named this section in honor of his prompt and responsible act of self-diagnosis.* I suggest you carefully examine the accompanying chart (*see Fig. 12, p. 146*). That should help you to keep hold of your good health before it forces you to leave the band.

This Is Shit

So you are keeping mind, soul, and body together with your sensible discipline. What next? Unhappiness and boredom of course . . .

I Want to Go Home

You've been away for eleven weeks. You can barely keep your eyes open. The back of your throat is permanently coated in bitter stomach acid because you vomit habitually before going on stage. In your perpetually daydreaming, unhinged state, you have become convinced that your partner at home is having an affair with your best friend because you got a text about them going for a drink together (conveniently ignoring the fact you have had carnal knowledge of six people since your last phone conversation with him/her). You can't even tell if you're more jealous about the imagined indiscretion or the fact they were having a pint in your local bar. Oh, for glorious home. You can't even remember your address. So you are running your fingers over your passport and are about to book a flight and go AWOL.

---

* It actually turned out to be to tonsillitis, so the move was even wiser. It also led to one of the greatest features in the history of music journalism (see www .manzanera.com/roxyarchive/imacnme3.htm). A truculent Bryan Ferry interviewed in monogrammed pajamas, drinking champagne in his hospital bed. If you are forced to put out the throat infection press release, you might as well do it in style.

Figure 12. The Bryan Ferry Self-Diagnosis "Throat Infection" Thermometer

Emergency Hospitalization

Symptoms: Being about to die

Causes: Serious raging illness going untreated. Probably brought on by all the stages below.

Cure: A month off. Proper medical attention. And an agreement in writing from the rest of the band that they won't replace you while you're gone, or ever, ever begin sentences in the future, "I know it's not your *fault* that you got appendicitis/had a heart attack, but imagine if we'd done the rest of that tour..."

Nervous Exhaustion

Symptoms: Falling over unexpectedly and not knowing where you are when you wake up

Causes: Ignoring all the stages below and just fighting the symptoms with dangerous drugs

Cure: Stomach pump, a couple of days off in a darkened room under an ice pack being fed grapes by someone you've found to look after you

Erratic Behavior

Symptoms: Spacey-ness and forgetfulness beyond your normal behavioral patterns —particularly regarding which song you're supposed to be playing next/now

Causes: Over-indulgence, chronic, fatigue, and even more chronic boredom

Cure: A week of proper detox, exercise, proper food, sleep, and a bunch of new records

Lethargy

Symptoms: Not wanting to get up in the morning/feeling destroyed

Causes: Junk food (call it an "addiction" if you're Craig Nichols from the Vines), a body stuffed full of toxins, and no proper sleep for three and a half months

Cure: Less shit food, a couple of vitamin tablets, a bit of fresh air, and a day or two off the sauce

Throat Infection

Symptoms: Sore/tight throat

Causes: Anything from eight hundred cigarettes a day and staying up till four every night shouting in noisy clubs to abject terror on seeing the huge tour itinerary land in your in-box.

Cure: For the former, lots of rest and hot honey and lemon, and if necessary a couple of days in bed. For the latter, pulling yourself together

Such lonely moments are to be expected. But going home is not an option. First go and find the person you get on best with, or the most personable member of the band, and talk to them. If they're not around, call everyone you know—it will still be cheaper than the flight. If it's the middle of the night where you are, or at home, there is only one course of action left.

Pull yourself to-fucking-gether and remember how lucky you are, you ungrateful bastard! You're in a band. One that's good enough and popular enough to tour. Imagine if you had to commute for an hour every day, among the gray faces on suburban trains—your only treats to look forward to being a couple of crafty hours on the Internet, with your equally work-weary chums and a couple of stiff anesthetizing drinks in the evening.

Knowing that, even if you do work late every night and climb the greasy pole, all you'll end up with is a slightly better lifestyle and no time or energy to enjoy it. *Your* working day on the other hand involves an hour and a half in front of a sweaty, adoring crowd, or messing about in recording studios. Keep that up for five "grueling" years and you'll be set up for life. Especially if you write some of the songs. Now grab those sleeping tablets or a little shot of Jack Daniel's and go to bed.

I'm Bored

It's come up in passing on virtually every page of this book, so it can't have come as a surprise—being in a band is often very, very dull indeed. If you're not counting down miles of highway or clouds, you're answering the same old questions to yet another journalist who isn't really listening to your answers and who will probably just chuck your quotes in their standard interview feature template.[*]

---

[*] I never do this.

Even worse, you just might be sitting idle while the singer and guitarist go through it without you.

The best thing to do is sneak off for a wander round town (having first checked whether there are any areas you really shouldn't set foot in). Even better, grab a floating PR person, record company skivvy, or bored journalist and get them to show you where all the second-hand clothes boutiques, record shops, and peculiar bars are to be found. You have to remember that you are visiting places you would most likely never have come to if you weren't in a band. That could be Northampton, of course, but it might also be L.A. You might as well take advantage and see the sights while you're there. Though if your band's look is androgynous/dirty/confrontational/silly/very gay, there might be certain destinations where it's a better idea to stay in your room and count the tiles in the bathroom.

If you are stuck indoors, try some games. Why not try the real-life version of children's board game favorite *Guess Who?* Pick a person in the room and make the others guess which one it is you're thinking of, with questions like "Male or female?" "Are they fat?" "Have they got a shit moustache?" etc. Don't play this game too loud, though. Or in truck stops in the American Midwest (or even Little Chef in Wolverhampton if the tour isn't that glamorous). Or why not try counting and classifying Goths? Remember the last section, it's still far less of a drag than doing a real job.

There Are Some Good Points to Being a Semi-Famous Professional Musician

Don't let all this negative talk put you off. I am just preparing you for the worst so that, as in all the previous chapters, when it starts to feel a tiny bit like you're actually being asked to work for a living, you don't suddenly panic. Being relatively responsible and disciplined should not be allowed to get in the way of you enjoying yourselves.

You can't just be dull, music-playing automatons or you'll have no ridiculous stories to impress your friends with when you get home. Even Muse have some fun on the road. Or say they do. I'm just steering you down a path of balance to avoid you breaking the band up before you even get to the second album.

Finally, America

With this in mind, here is the final touring warning. And it's mainly directed at British bands. When British bands get to tour America they usually respond in a couple of ways. Either they recoil at the sheer hard work and crowd-pleasing sweat it takes to break the place on a gigantic coast-to-coast tour. Or they fall hopelessly in love with it (well, New York and California anyway) and decide they want to live there. If they are also the songwriters, that means a sudden jolt toward Springsteen, rootsy rock 'n' roll, and songs that mention American place names.[*] It's probably best to try and stop them.

Not that is *has* to be America.[†] Travel can, even under the circumstances of doing it as part of a touring band, broaden the mind. Or at least make you want to move to the other side of the world. Particularly if album two is expected soon. The point is that touring can be a powerful catalyst in making people hanker for a dramatic change of lifestyle. Ignore them till you get home, then if they still want to emigrate, say you'll do it too after the third album (even though it's a lie) and see if it helps to soothe their itchy feet.

You can now tour with confidence, relatively safe in the knowledge that when you come back you will still be, and still want to be, a member of the band that set off.

---

[*] Americans themselves aren't even immune. Look at the Killers' second album.

[†] There is hilarious footage of a kaftan-bedecked Ginger Baker of Cream learning drumming methods in an African village in the late sixties; looking utterly terrifying in his mind-opened percussive zeal.

So What Have We Learned?

- If you list yourselves in alphabetical order on your MySpace page, you are doomed to failure
- Your lawyer is there to keep you warm
- Wearing shades at Christmas dinner is a sure sign that the press will destroy your next album
- The keys to happy touring are Post-it Notes, underwear, and Tylenol

4

THE DIFFICULT SECOND ALBUM,
AND BEYOND

Anyone ready to make the next album then? This question will already be pressing at your drink-bruised temples before your bags have grazed the pile of dusty, unopened mail congealing behind your front door on your return home.

And the answer is simple. No. You are drained and disorientated. Right now you have as much hope of writing your magisterial second album as you do of still being awake by *Gossip Girl*. You need a rest. More important, the only life you have experienced over the last eighteen months has been among the brash, forecasting chatter of the music industry. Which is far less interesting as a source of musical inspiration than getting dumped or the depressing nature of your hometown or whatever your debut disc was about.

You need a moment to regain your slim hold on reality. Great songs only appear when you and the band feel charged and indestructible, and have something to say. And right now, staring into the mirror over the sink, into your entertainment-hollowed eyes, temporarily unaware of the gushing tap and all life around you, you don't really feel very charged or indestructible at all. And you certainly have nothing to say. You want to just phone your mom for a bit of comfort but feel too indefinably sickened by yourself to dial the number.

In days of yore, you'd have been frog-marched down to the studio to get another album in Woolworths by Christmas. Even if that meant filling it with tepid cover versions mainly played by session musicians. This is not how it will be for you. In days of yore, you wouldn't have had to spend the best part of two years recording, touring, and selling the first album. Things were simpler. Buses had conductors, people wore hats, and the music industry wasn't such a sprawling part of the world's lifestyle marketing machine (though it was just as nasty). In days of yore you could also get away with more inferior albums—no one would have expected your "career" to last as long as two years, anyway. So those two years would have been spent piling the shelves with product before your own little teen fashion bubble burst.

But even for you, outside there is still a whirlwind—record companies planning marketing campaigns and tie-in invite-only promotional shows, block-bookings being made in expensive residential recording studios, hire bills from the last tour landing on your manager's desk and being ignored with a gulp. Even strangers coming up to you in bars and asking what your new songs are like. Aarrgggh—what are you going to do?

Fuck 'em. The only record you're about to make will be one that eclipses your first from every conceivable angle. There will be no disappointing sophomore efforts from you. Not on my watch. This chapter will tell you how to do it. And that takes a lot more than heading for the studio and jamming a few meandering riffs, half-checking your phone for messages from your latest squeeze while autopiloting solos. No, it's more hard work I'm afraid, and this time it even gets emotional.[*]

Sex, Drugs, and Rock 'n' Roll

You must make the next album amazing. And that starts with getting your lives back in order. My guess is that they're currently a bit of a mess. When did you last see your parents? Your friends? When did you last even feel that overbearing urge to write a song? When did you last have any kind of normal perspective on anything at all? You have built a dam in your lives and some of the water needs to be drained out. Not filled even higher till the pressure cracks it (probably somewhere in the middle of an argument about backing vocals while recording the next album).

And what is this bulging water menace of which I talk? Mainly sex, drugs, and rock 'n' roll—the lifestyle objectives to which any responsible musician is expected to devote his or her free time, and the next source of bandalism you're likely to run into. They act as magnets, pulling you all as individuals away from the center of the band. If you don't halt this process, the unity you built up and kept hold of in the first three chapters will be lost.

But these are very broad categories, so let me clarify. In the case of bandalism, sex, drugs, and rock 'n' roll translate as the following:

- Sex—the settling, unsettling, or just downright distracting influence of romantic love or compulsive, hedonistic sluttishness

---

[*] Don't worry—not too emotional—not as much as Dave Mustaine in Metallica's *Some Kind of Monster* film opening his heart to drummer Lars Ulrich about having felt like a failure for the twenty years since he got kicked out of the band. It won't get that bad till chapter 5.

- Drugs—the physical or mental collapse and erratic behavior provoked by addictions
- Rock 'n' Roll—the exclusive, roped-off VIP existence of the modern-day minor-rock celebrity

The effects of any of these are likely to make going straight back into the studio futile. You need to repair yourselves. And crucially you need to do it in private. As far as anyone outside the band is concerned, you're writing album two. You don't want the record company striding in, bullying you and ruining this deeply necessary stock-take. Those of you yawning at the back and mechanically chopping out lines at this point are the ones most in need, so pay attention.

To aid you in this tricky time, I have predicted the effects that sex, drugs, and rock 'n' roll will have had on you and divided you up by the personality types from the quiz in chapter 1. And if you're going to divine people's future by crudely breaking them down into a few broad personality types, what better way to do it than a horoscope? Here, then, is each member's sex, drugs, and rock 'n' roll horoscope. Read the ones that relate to all the members of your band. If you are aware of each other's weak spots in advance, you will be in a better position to avoid trouble or, more realistically, deal with it when it comes your way:

The Horoscopes

First, here's a quick reminder of the categories:
A—The Natural Leader
B—The Artist
C—The Quiet One
D—The Lairy-Mad-for-It Lunatic

A+B—The Hustler

A+C—The Backseat Driver

A+D—The Cool One

B+C—The Moody One

B+D—The Self-Destructive Genius

C+D—The Enthusiastic Amateur

The Natural Leader

Sex

You're a confident and charismatic type. People would probably be prepared to sleep with you even if you weren't in a band. You need have little fear of hopelessly falling for the first person who will look after you and ditching the band to be with them. Depending on your tastes, the only waves your sex life will cause in the band are due to jealousy—either for your prodigious sexual conquests or your stable, well-adjusted relationship.

Drugs

You could be in more danger here. Particularly when it comes to stimulants. The sheer irritation you could cause the other members with even more self-confidence would be enough to break any band up. But no doubt your sense of balance will protect you from anything worse than a few lost weekends.

Rock 'n' Roll

This is your Achilles heel. In the course of endless exclusive parties you will become bloated on vol-au-vents, self-importance, and people agreeing with you all the time. Your increasing love of the sound of your own voice, especially when it's in conversation with beautiful, famous people, could have a disastrous effect on its singing cousin. And we all know what's going to win out when it comes to a choice between working on some lyrics about social alienation or chatting up TV presenters at an ultrahip gallery opening. The more righteous among you may eschew such empty headed socializing and be up to your knees in good causes before you can say Bob Geldof. In that case substitute chatting up TV presenters for talking to Nelson Mandela or gallery openings for organizing meetings about climate change. The effect will still be the same.

The Artist

Sex

Oh dear. Let's look at this as damage limitation. You're a sensitive soul. For you, relationships are likely to be tempestuous affairs. You'll most likely fall in love with someone wildly inappropriate. Either they will treat you terribly (according to you), or embroil you in some kind of seedy lifestyle (requiring little persuasion on your part). Whichever way, one double bleep on your phone and the band will get no sense out of you for weeks. And for the band, they just need to be patient. Don't bother confronting. You will drop them in seconds for a deep-seeming love but come running back when it all goes wrong. More hopefully, you'll actually find someone to look after you and the band will breathe a sigh of relief. Failing that, you'll slip into a peculiar and slightly bitter asexual vacuum.

Drugs

Oh dear again. Things that excite the senses are, as a rule, quite a favorite of yours. That's why you like music. Are addicted to it almost. You also love music because it makes the world go away. So, by nature, you're an addictive escapist. Fucking hell . . .

Rock 'n' Roll

You'll do the rounds of the parties and exclusive gigs—mainly on the look out for love or intoxication, but you're not all that sociable really. You get bored and restless. You might get a bit loud. And if there are other people in a room who are more important than you, you'll start to feel a bit odd. The sort of odd that leads to a punch up or a stomach pump. Either way, it's a night in casualty and a week of engagements canceled through nervous exhaustion. You'll soon tire of going out much. Then you're in even more danger, when you stay in going quietly mad. It's the rest of the band's duty to stop this happening before you overheat and forget how to write songs.

The Quiet One
Sex
Oh, come on, you've got nothing to worry about. You'll just be like a normal person, only you'll get more interest because you're in a band. You'll probably be married before the second album anyway. To someone you were already going out with when you joined the band. You'd never be interested in groupies. Except to make mental notes of some of the funny things they said. Well . . . until the money roles in and you get used to a glamorous lifestyle. Then you'll go off the rails for a bit till your original spouse rescues you.

Drugs
If there is a problem for you, it's most likely to be here. Mainly because if you get seriously addicted to anything, no one will actually notice until you overdose. They'll just think you've been being slightly more quiet than normal. And you'll be too embarrassed to let anyone know you're in trouble. More likely, though, you'll just find people a bit dull when they're out of it and go and find some other ones to talk to.

Rock 'n' Roll
You'll like the aftershows and the VIP areas. You'll be amused—walking round sparkling rooms—that you ever came to be invited. Much like being in a band, you quite like seeing glitz up close but not really getting involved. Unless you find some old record producer to chat with at the bar about reverb chambers of old, you'll be home in bed by 2:00 a.m. Your only danger is that other members of the band will be jealous of your affable popularity.

The Lairy-Mad-for-It Lunatic

Sex

Making drunken lunges at people and being pushed away in disgust is most likely as close as you come to this category. Or more sordid encounters. The band probably need not fear you ditching them for true love.

Drugs

Without wanting to psychoanalyze you too much, there must be a reason why you have to keep everything crazy and drunk. Some void that needs filling. Whatever that is, being in a band, there will be more than enough people around you to keep it filled for free with booze and drugs until you die. For the band, it's bad enough when you mess up gigs and recordings because you're fucked up. But that's nothing to when you're coming down/back up and morose. Your mood swings will not make you popular. If you don't die young, it might turn out it was all just youthful high spirits. Then you'll mellow with age (thirty) into the peculiar, balanced dignity of the faded hell-raiser.

Rock 'n' Roll

You'll get terribly overexcited around real life celebrities. Not because of them, just because of the atmosphere. But the rest of the band will soon make sure you don't find out about events once you've pissed in the champagne one too many times (i.e., once). Still this won't stop you showing up plastered and causing mayhem and criminal damage till dawn.

The Hustler

Sex

You love intensely. You do everything pretty intensely. But as everything you do happens in erratic bursts of energy, it won't be a problem for the band. No sooner have you made a grand romantic gesture of commitment to someone than you'll be on the phone to the manager at 3:00 a.m. with an idea for a T-shirt you want to get printed before tomorrow night's gig. The only trouble for the band where your love life is concerned will be feeling sympathy for your put upon partner and guilty about having to cover up all your rampant infidelity.

Drugs

You'll have your dabbles and your wobbles but you'll be fine. Your short attention span makes you largely immune to addiction, while your peculiarly robust constitution lets you off most of the after-effects. Besides, you're far too self-reliant to cause the band any long-term worries. Spontaneously deciding to leave or insisting doggedly on stupid ideas while under the influence will just be a permanent reality for them to get used to.

Rock 'n' Roll

You'll turn up to the guest-list bashes, have a laugh for a bit, then go on somewhere else. Despite your love of all things brash, you're not that into it in other people. You lack the diligence for social climbing, though you'll still doubtless charm a lot of people with your hyperintense energy levels. The band will not lose you to the pages of *Heat*.

The Backseat Driver

Sex

Like all A's, charisma and self-confidence stop this being a problem for you. Though unlike the other A's, in your case, everyone but you will find this confusing. Knowing you only as the traffic warden of good times, the band will react with endless taunts and jibes about how someone like you could be attractive to anyone at all. You will take it in good grace, secretly knowing that you're in charge here. This will annoy the others even more.

Drugs

Your main drug problem will be your heavy-handed attempts at enforced rehab on the rest of the band. Imagine it from their point of view—not just being fed horrible medicine but being fed it by a teacher. They will hate you, they will rebel, but ultimately you'll probably save one of their lives. And never let them forget it.

Rock 'n' Roll

You're a bit of a social climber. Though you were probably on a higher rung than the rest of the band even at the start. Like the Leader, socializing might be your undoing. Though it won't be due to not putting the work in with the band. Rather, the work you put in will be increasingly geared toward capturing the hearts of whichever social milieu you fancy swanning around in next. You won't get sucked in as far as the Leader because, frankly, the people you try to ingratiate yourself with won't much trust you and will like you even less. But you'll be sure to irritate the whole band with deliberate name-dropping at every opportunity.

The Cool One

Sex

Not really the kind of thing you get hung up about to be honest. You're never lacking a line of people who are prepared to throw themselves at you. There are far more interesting reasons for you to fail to turn up to work than just a day in bed.

Drugs

A funny one this. You can be uncharacteristically loutish when the mood takes you. And the mood for a bit of chemical excess may well tempt you quite often. The chances are the rest of the band won't even be party to it. You could be on crack and they'd only find out later from someone else. The biggest problem is likely to be some of your more easily led bandmates trying to copy you.

Rock 'n' Roll

Put you in a room full of glamorous people and no one will see you for a week. While the others are trying to move in on pretty publicists, you'll have somehow been invited into a private inner sanctum. The credit cards will come out and two days later you'll return full of vague stories of fascinating characters and exclusive locations. Don't be too surprised if after this the others seem really interested but then get really edgy and spend the next few hours accusing you of "playing like shit."

The Moody One

Sex

Due to your inbuilt love of moral self-righteousness and martyrdom, you will not desert the band for the sake of love. This does not mean an easy ride for your colleagues though. You will remind them all of your sacrifices for the band, pointedly talking to the manager after gigs while the others go on a hunt for thrills. The truth is that those interested in the more casual encounter might give you a bit of a wide berth, smelling trouble. Another source of veiled resentment. Even if you are a broodingly handsome Moody One, you'll still find something to complain about.

Drugs

You're a snob, really. In a nice way. Either you're aggressively straightedge, or rather a refined connoisseur of chemistry as a means to enlightenment. Either way, you're more likely to be giving lectures than receiving them. If the others were not so crass about it all they might end up less of a mess.

Rock 'n' Roll

Prepare for evenings making awkward conversation on the edge of groups. Your total suspicion of (not to mention disgust at) artifice and sham occasionally making you come across as a bit rude and difficult. No one will have any trouble tearing you away from the finger buffet for a night of work. And if the others show signs of distraction or excess the next day, you'll be sure to make them aware of it. As for them, if they can get used to tiptoeing around your little personal rug of eggshells, they will have little trouble from your dealings with the outside world.

The Self-Destructive Genius
Sex
As we already know, any collision between you and the outside world is potentially volatile, possessing as you do equal measures of passionate vulnerability and recklessness. So this is really a guide for how the rest of the band can look after you. Let them hope that whoever you fall for will share some of that burden with them. With any luck, that person will help you mellow, though that might spell disaster for your songs. Otherwise expect to be heartbreaker and heartbroken in bafflingly quick succession.

Drugs
Yes. Lots of them. You won't be able to resist. Booze and cigarettes alone could do you all kinds of shaky, unstabilizing damage. As with love, fingers must be crossed that you'll mellow. Drugs aren't even likely to be much of a creative tool to you. More just an internal fortress against feelings of helplessness. The very helplessness that, while it makes you miserable, helps you write those amazing songs. The rest of you beware. This could end tragically. I hope there's a Backseat Driver among you.

Rock 'n' Roll
This is obvious already. Either frequent disheveled appearances in the tabloids or open hostility toward the phony demimonde of rock stardom. Either will lead to an intense reaction and much antagonism between you and the rest of the band. Who will no doubt fail to understand why you behave the way you do.

The Enthusiastic Amateur
Sex
After a very short time you will get used to being the stepping-stone over which other people get to the famous members of the band. Not that you'll really care. You'll get a lot more interest than you would have otherwise, and those people's motivation won't be all that dissimilar to yours in joining the band. You're quite a stable sort really. Certainly plagued by far fewer of the precious commitment issues that cloud the rest of the band's love lives. You'll probably just find a nice person and stick with them.

Drugs
Well you'll have your moments—you have to don't you if you're in a band? Though it's quite unlikely it will be much of a brain shattering experience, or even a painfully addictive one. It's just having fun, having a laugh— nothing to get obsessed with. Unless things get tough and you start to feel insecure that you don't deserve to be in the band. Then that source of escapism might prove rather more inviting. You'll be okay, though. In fact you'll be touched and surprised by just how quickly everyone rallies around you. Even the Moody One. They need your stability more than they let you realize.

Rock 'n' Roll
You just won't be invited to things all that much. It won't be the band's fault, people will just forget you exist. You don't much like small talk anyway, and feel much more comfortable around your real friends. You'll probably have more real friends than the rest of the band put together, anyway. Even real friends in the industry. And when you do meet fashionable or important people you are likely to say something wrong, or insult someone, or fall over, and you will never live it down.

———

Armed with these predictions and warnings, you can all be prepared for what's coming. The unexpected is bewildering and chaotic, the predictable merely a nuisance. But this is only the first stage of the healing process that will make album two so great. Once you have worked out what condition touring has spat you out in, the knives will come out—a bloodbath of power-hungry back-stabbing. And don't think that being in a nice band will excuse you this stage. That will just make it all more underhand.

Firing People

If the band is facing one of the difficult situations above with a member, the likely first reaction is to reach for the big, flashing switch marked "fire." We will come on to members leaving of their own volition in the next chapter, but for now, we need to look at members being pushed. And when I say "look at," I mean, "tell you why in almost all cases it's a really fucking stupid idea."

There are many situations in which you feel the band could do without someone's sniping, moaning, or rampant, personality-leeching substance abuse. Marching them off the plank back into the unforgiving waters of real life can feel like a fair and just punishment and a convenient way to leave your troubles behind. But replacing someone will not solve all of the band's problems. It will just make them different and probably worse.

The expression "better the devil you know" is never more aptly deployed than when talking about band lineups. That bastard chemistry probably has you handcuffed to this loser for eternity. If you kick someone out you risk losing the magic formula between you all forever. Firing is a last resort and you must try every possible solution before you settle on it. All seven of them.

The Firing Spiral

Let's think for a second. What are you trying to do? Make a brilliant second album—nothing more or less. And what does that require? Well you know that from the first two chapters—a band that all the members want to be in, that feels unstoppable and in which all members are willing and able to do their bit to make a charge toward pop infinity. All other considerations—ego, personal hygiene, playing ability, defects of temper, and personality—are irrelevant if they don't directly undermine that ideal.

All you need is a great band. And if this member was integral to that the first time, why do you suddenly think you can do it without them now? Firing someone cannot be done lightly—each person is far too fundamental to what makes the band great. So if there is a member lined up in the cross-hairs, you have to follow all of the stages in the Firing Spiral chart (*see Fig. 13, p. 166*) before you pull the trigger. Each one gives you a chance to solve the problem and keep the band intact.

Figure 13. The Firing Spiral

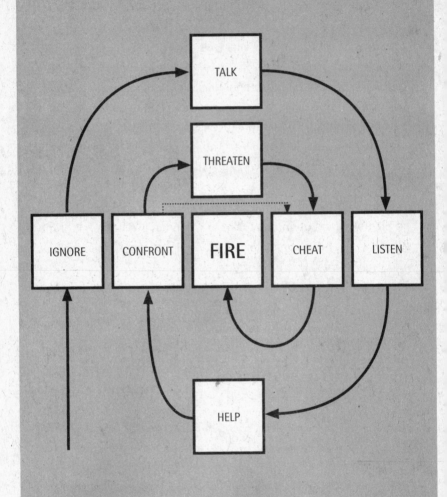

Figure 13. The Firing Spiral Notes

IGNORE

First, just ignore the problem—their surliness, their lack of interest, their terrible playing—and hope they sort it out for themselves. Is it actually damaging the band, or have they always been like that?

TALK

If that's not getting very far, bring the problem up. Tell them why you're worried/pissed off. It's up to you and your band how you approach it, but if voices raise and doors slam off their hinges you probably got it wrong. Telling them there's a problem gives them a chance to correct it

LISTEN

It might also provoke a torrent of dissatisfied bile and spleen, directed at you. Perhaps it isn't them ruining the band, but you with your anal, control-freak pickiness. Listen to them. They might be right. Alternatively they may be drunk, telling you this between gushes of vomit, during a confused waking dawn. In that case, it's time for stage four.

HELP

Yes. Actually help them. Book them into rehab, or drumming lessons or anger management classes, or whatever's required. This band was great because they were a part of it. It's as much in your interests as theirs to get them back to normal.

CONFRONT

If, in response to this, they try to escape, or plaster rude slogans on your guitars, you need to confront them about all the stupid things they're doing to destroy the band. You are allowed to pin them over a table and scream this in their face if necessary.

THREATEN

They're still ignoring the problem? Explain calmly and rationally everything you have just bawled emotionally—why you can't work with them at the minute, why they need to remember how to tune a guitar. Then stop and hiss that unless things change, it's over for them. Don't do this if you're a jovial person or given to regular peculiar pronouncements—leave it to one of the nastier/more normal members of the band.

CHEAT

Of course ultimatums are always a risk. Ideally, at the same time you'll be rehearsing potential replacements. If it feels as good with new players, especially on new songs, your recalcitrant member is as good as fired. This is very unlikely. More normally it will all feel rather flat and you'll have to hope threatening worked.

FIRE

If you come this far, they don't want to be in the band anyway, which means you are left with no choice but to send them on their way with best wishes and a carriage clock. You might want to check "Losing a Member" in the final chapter for a few tips on what to do next.

Trouble at the Top

That's all very well if it's the second keyboard player causing the problems—someone who doesn't seem superficially integral to the band. Someone you can actually fire. But what about if the complications are all at the top? What if it's the singer or the main songwriter who seems, temporarily, to have lost their place in the plot? Then it gets really tricky.

Wait On

Look, hang on a minute. Where's all this leader shit come from? We're a band. We decide things as a band. We don't have a fucking leader! It's not Arthur Snodgrass and His Tepid Five, we're a proper band.

Really? When it comes to deciding what the next album's going to sound like, no one holds any more sway than the rest of you? No one grabs, or has more responsibility heaped on them when it comes to big decisions? No one writes most of the songs, or directs things in the studio? No one plans your career more than the rest of you? Talks to the manager and the record company more? Brilliant. Move on to the next section then.

For the rest of you, and believe me, you are the normal ones, I'll assume such responsibilities aren't always so equally shared. And whether you're the person, or one of the people, in charge, or just the one who drinks tea till someone needs a bass line, you all need to be aware of what might be happening among the band's decision makers. Because what happens with them could have a dramatic bearing on the next record.

Here are a few of the most common ways in which leadership unravels and some ideas for solutions:

The Leader Is Squeezing the Rest of You Out

It's a recurring theme so far. Heads swelled with success, now is often the time when your resident songwriter/loudmouth starts to forget that it took a team effort to get you here. Suddenly no one is allowed to question their half-formed new songs or horrible new beard. And after months and months of watching them being recognized, feted, and interviewed, you almost start to believe them too. Especially, if you're afraid they might run off for a solo career and leave you all screwed.

You need to surgically remove their newly grown rogue ego. You need to remind them very forcibly of just what a team effort this band must continue to be. And this is not done best through confrontation. Or the other common band mistake (the Faces, the Band, and many others) of just dropping the quantity and quality off your contributions in a sulk to teach the singer/famous guy a lesson (after all, if you sorted the publishing out earlier like I told you to, you will be getting a proper reward for what you put in). So the best reaction is to attack them with positivity—with hundreds of great musical ideas and group collaborations. Humble them with the power of your contributions. Excitable alternative suggestions will get you far further in keeping a more equal influence over the band's future than whiny griping. Unless . . .

The Leader Has an Agenda

It usually comes like a free toy in a cereal box with the above problem. Due to a lust for power, celebrity or a cooler or bigger audience, the leader starts to put their interests above the band's. In particular it often happens when they have one greedy eye on a solo career on the other side.

If you start to feel that you are being used as the overture to a solo record, you could always confront the leader angrily and demand that they focus back on the band. But ultimatums from a position of weakness only lead to war or humiliation. Usually both, one after the other. So, unlike my last suggestion of wholesome positive energy, if you feel like you're being used, you'll have to do some judicious using of your own in return.

If you trust them not to screw up the music on the way, then just take advantage of the leader's self-seeking energy and enjoy your time in the slipstream. If you think, though, that they are about to drive you off a musical cliff for the sake of their ego, you might have to try and outflank them. They want to go all tasteless and stadium? Fine, go along with it. But in the meantime, start collaborating outside the band with the far cooler artists you think you should be sounding like. A couple of features on you in the press and people referring to you as the real brains behind the operation and they may well divert a bit more energy back to the band and your ideas. Especially if they think they can rob a bit of your newly found credibility along the way.

I'll admit it's a risk, they could equally just use your outside dalliances as an excuse to finally get working on that solo record. But even this might work in your favor. Statistically speaking, the solo records made by people in bands are almost universally shit. Letting them fail in their own name may be enough to win back their interest. And if, by some chance, they do succeed and run off, you will at least have made steps toward a post band career of your own. A hollow victory perhaps, but that's always better than a defeat.

If you try to fight them at every turn and go sulky, the next album will be miserable, fall between two stools, and sink all of your careers.

The Leader's Gone Nuts/The Leader's Gone Missing

So that's fine if you're dealing with a power hungry leader pushing you toward their vision of the future. But what about the other alternative? Alarmed at the monster they have helped to create, terrified of where to go next, or just ruined by sleep-deprivation and drugs, your leader might choose now to start exhibiting all the outward characteristics of being a great big mentalist. Erratic behavior, stupid ideas, constantly changing their mind, demanding that you augment the lineup of your jangly indie band with a rapper called Dave—whom he met busking outside a station. All pretty fair signs that the leader has misplaced his or her marbles.*

How you respond rather depends what condition said leader is in. If they're looking bad, perhaps you should try to get them into rehab or pack them off to their mom's for a couple of weeks to ease the pressure. Though if they are genuinely suffering with a form of mental illness, curing it is a notoriously tricky task— one that human thought has yet to master conclusively. So it might be a bit of a tall order for the bassist and drummer from the Figz, or whomever you are. But, however you do it and whatever the cause of their problems, they need help. They do not need you poking them in the ribs and saying, "Where's the new songs, mad boy?"

But such level-headed wisdom is not always the right path for bands and their creativity. So instead, maybe you could try joining them—eagerly following wherever their peculiar new inspiration is taking them. Primal Scream had been through sixties harmony pop and seventies dirty rock 'n' roll when frontman Bobby Gillespie suddenly got turned on to ecstasy, clubbing, and the burgeoning acid house scene. A more lily-livered band might have kept their

---

* Maybe add to that building a tepee in their living room, lying in the dark listening to the chorus of the Ronettes "Be My Baby" on loop for four hours or making a big sandpit to put their piano in, all of which Brian Wilson of the Beach Boys did.

knuckles tight around their guitars and run with them to the hills. But they were made of equally odd stuff. They threw themselves into the reinvention, teaming up with DJ/producer/remixer/journalist Andy Weatherall to make their first (and indeed only) truly great record, *Screamadelica*. Think what a crappy musical legacy they might have left behind were it not for that one collective, "Fuck it, let's see what happens . . ."

In other cases, joining in can be a really bad idea. The other guitarists in the first, blues lineup of Fleetwood Mac threw themselves all too vigorously into the wake of axe-genius Peter Green, following him into drugs, insanity, religious cults, and sketch-out disappearing acts. My advice, then, if you are going to follow, hang on to your hats . . .

Coups

The other potential result of the missing/fucked-up leader scenario is the headless band. The leader lies slumped in a haze, not even producing weird ideas but coming up with none at all. No one knows what to do, everyone panics. The drummer starts writing songs (always the most spine-chilling alarm bell), and there is a high chance of a coup. Power is not notoriously fond of a vacuum. Frozen in fear, the stricken leader may find that other people in the band are more than happy to relieve them of the pressure (and glory) of their role.

Lowell George of Little Feat lost control of his own band. A rabid musical perfectionist, especially in the studio, he started as their principal songwriter and creative lynchpin. Unfortunately his studio perfectionism had two side effects—a need for stimulants to keep him going all night dubbing tracks, and a tendency to limit the involvement of the other members on the records. So when the latter had annoyed them and the former started to weaken his creative powers, keyboard player Bill Payne and his sidekick, guitarist Paul Barrere jumped in. They filled the song gap with modish synth workouts and dragged the band from funky country to labored jazz-rock in the space of a couple of albums. Unfortunately, for George, the band finally started selling records too. So the coup was to the lasting benefit of their bank balances, but to the lasting discredit of their musical credibility.

Power battles in bands are usually won with songwriting. Brian Jones may have formed the Rolling Stones, but once Mick and Keith had been locked in a room by the manager, Andrew Loog Oldham, and forced to write songs (in a conscious decision to rival Lennon and McCartney), they rapidly assumed control. Indeed, in the five years from 1964 to 1969, Jones went from nominal leader, via losing lead guitar duties and his girlfriend to Keith, to being kicked out of the band. That's ruthless stuff.

So the lesson for the ailing leaders? If you're losing your band, you need to write some songs. And don't just rattle off a bunch of crappy ones. If someone else has an eye on your position, they'll use that to add further weight to the argument that you're greening round the edges and approaching your sell by date. And once you've lost control, it's very hard to get it back again. You might find yourself perpetually marginalized within the band, regardless of whether you regain your brilliance later. Because by then, those who ousted you will be far too comfortable to give back power without a scrap.

So is a coup a problem? It depends how good the replacement leadership is. Whatever their gifts, a coup tends to create a totally different band from the one that formed. As we know already, tampering with your chemistry is a bit stupid. Even if there is no lineup change, just shifting the band hierarchy and focus can give it a totally different identity. Well, a slightly different and often less good one. And if the magic disappears, so usually does the quality of the band.

Dual Leaders

This is all assuming that you only have one leader in the band. That's often not the case. Much as any band's brilliance is drawn from human interaction, so a band's leadership can be best if the leader's crown is bobbing about on the waves between two members. Two self-important loudmouths can be better than one. There are clear benefits to this—the division of labor, if you want to put it that way. One person can make things happen in the press while the other makes them happen in the studio. Or both can be good at the same things but enhance each other's contributions. For example, the solid good sense of one can cancel out the stupidity of the other, while the latter's better taste can limit the former's granny-targeted banality. Yes, we know which famous band I mean here. Whether they fight or lean on each other, two leaders can cover the gaps in each others energy and share the stress of keeping the band moving forwards.

But when things are going wrong, they can also rip it asunder in a bitter war for power and territory. If it comes to this point, the rest of the band may ally themselves to one or other of them. Like children with a favorite parent, they will huddle against the one who indulges them most. In a band with an even number of members, that means stalemate. Not a word often associated with the creation of trailblazing art. Even if the rest of the band just develops an "us" and "them" complex against the leaders, it's still bad news for the music. Ideas will start to be rejected not for being bad, but because they come from the wrong person.

So what can you do? If you are not the squabbling leaders, you could always down tools until they sort themselves out. Forget loyalty, if they're selfish enough to risk the band for their ego-fighting, you should be self-preserving enough to use the same methods to them snap out of it. With any luck, and in a band keen to maintain at least some level of creative quality, the threat of (non)industrial (in)action might be enough to make your warring leaders talk to each other, especially if you make that the sole condition of your return.

And for the leaders themselves? They need to bond again. And very, very rapidly. Whatever the band and whomever you are, I can give those leaders one piece of infallible advice: on your own you will be shit—shadows of your former glory. Find a way to work together properly or you will never make a good record again. I have seen Babyshambles. I have seen Dirty Pretty Things. If you want to split up, split up, but you are probably throwing away the magic forever—even if you overcome your conflicts and reform later (I have seen the Tears). Rent a cottage in the Hebrides. Leave your phones behind. Just take yourselves and some guitars. If you both come back alive and together you can make this work. The rest of you, if you want to do something useful, book the cottage, drive them there, and lie about it if you have to.

Only when these personality issues are addressed and the band has returned to some kind of balance is it time to begin work on the second album. And if you've just been through any of these problems, this should start with doing something to clear the stinking, rotten air.

At Last . . . the Difficult Second Album

It will have taken you all different levels of stress, time, and emotion to get here, but finally you find yourselves, bruised but intact, standing on the glistening threshold of album two. No doubt the Red Hot Chili Peppers would take this opportunity to have another of their bonding holidays. And it's not a bad idea. It depends how you're feeling about each other after the events of the last few pages. For some of you, the scars will only just be starting to heal. Ideally what you need to do next is return to the mood of chapter 2 and revisit the Rehearsal Methods section. Yet again, you need to begin by finding somewhere you can work together as a band, feel excited by the new project, and write thousands of songs. Something unusual and different is a good place to start. If, in your heads, you just see the words "MORE OF THE SAME UNTIL WE BREAK UP" flashing over the road ahead as the tour bus disappears into the sunset, this will not be the triumph it could be.

Getting It Together II

The Clash had a great idea for their second album. As they were huge reggae fans, they decided to go on a musical fact-finding mission to Jamaica and record there in the legendary Studio 1. As I say, this was a fine, fine idea—to take inspiration for their next move from the music they loved and do something new. Unfortunately, they made a crucial mistake. Only songwriters Joe Strummer and Mick Jones went. They left bassist Paul Simonon at home. He was the one who had arguably got them into reggae to start with. Not just mean but politically stupid.* Now is not the time to get hierarchical and divisive. If you want album two to be great, you must

---

* Not their only mistake of the trip. Somewhat ignorant of local gang culture, they also managed to offend a few people and ended up being chased out of the studio by men brandishing guns. And the second album proved to be a bit disappointing. They did far better on 1980's *Sandinista*, which they recorded in New York while absorbing the blossoming hip-hop scene.

include the whole band. There's not much point going off into new realms of influence if you haven't bothered letting the rhythm section know.

Still the intention was good; to freshen things up and move forward. To take the initiative—unlike their contemporaries the Jam. Just a couple of months after their first album they were packed off to a farmhouse in the middle of nowhere with a tape recorder to come up with the second one. They were aged between nineteen and twenty-two. They just got drunk. Such a Mike Oldfield setting was particularly inappropriate for a punk band. But even when they returned to spitting London to complete it, things were no better. They weren't really focused and didn't have enough time to work on the songs, as was obvious from the end product, the lumpy *This Is the Modern World*. Things were going the same way for album three only a matter of months after that (record companies really knew how to push bands in those days) until Paul Weller went home to his parents house for a bit and, undistracted, remembered all the things that made him write songs in the first place. The result was the fabulous *All Mod Cons*. However you choose to approach it, what you do next has to come from the band or at least be relevant to it—not from the stock (and cheap) ideas of the record company. Yes, I'm afraid you have to do a bit of work and think about it. You need to start work feeling as daringly confident in the end product as you did with the first album.

Songs

This starts with the songs. You need to write yourselves senseless. Don't start thinking that everything you do is good enough just because you're successful. Why would that be—you're still the same people.

During any given month in the career of any decent song-writer, the majority of the songs they write or start writing will be rubbish. If you decide to write fewer and fewer songs, because now you think you're Scott Walker and couldn't possibly write crap ones anymore, you will be well on the way to a terrible album. Either retreading the first or making a half-baked lunge for novelty—all with the quality control filter switched off. And don't just aim for writing the singles. If you do that, you'll make facsimiles of the ones from the first album, only missing the spark, spontaneity, and charm. Big, hollow, and overblown, sounding like reverberations of your diminished talent echoing off into space. Or "growers" as they're described.

An easy way to avoid that is to remember another part of the rehearsal methods from chapter 2. However big and important you are now, you still need some kind of feedback on your songs. It's no time to forget other people's opinions. Though it was their third album, Oasis's *Be Here Now* is a case in point. Recorded under conditions of near terrorist-cell secrecy, the tapes held back from all but their innermost inner sanctum, the album itself was an almost unmitigated musical disaster, permanently tarnishing their reputation, despite its high sales. We all know the truth, you only cover up bad things—farts, stains, and infidelities. If you're proud of what you're doing, you're desperate for the world to hear it instantly. How keen you feel to play your manager the demos for album two is a fairly reliable indicator of how good the new songs are. Until you've got some you're happy with, keep writing more. If you can find anyone vaguely unbiased or musically trust-worthy to consult, then all the better. In fact this should be the producer's job.

Songs You Wrote on the Road

There are no rules with any of this of course, but facts tend to show that the majority of songs written on the road are not worth writing. The reasons are fairly obvious. There are so many distractions and everyone's in more of a waiting about kind of mood than a taking a song and mauling it into shape one. Quite apart from the fact all your instruments might be in a cargo hold. Often the best time to write on the road is at night after a show, in that pleasing tinnitus haze when each chord you play seems to swell with a thousand possible melodies.* Unfortunately nighttime's precisely when all the fun's happening and it seems easier to leave the song half-finished and head for the bar.

Even worse, after a summer on the festival circuit, your new "songs" are likely to be weighted more heavily in favor of crowd-pleasing clap-along breakdowns than anything resembling a pass-able musical idea.

On the plus side, you can at least use your soundchecks to work out band arrangements for new material. If you're *really* into the songs you could even drop them into your actual set to see how they go down. But I'll tell you now if you like—muted appreciation. Either that or they won't quite gel, the audience will seem a bit restless and you'll end up dropping what could have been a really good song. People do not pay for tickets to see you to hear stuff they don't know.

There are some examples of songs in the very highest rock firma-ment being written on tour. The Beatles wrote "She Loves You" in a hotel room in Newcastle on a night off. Even the legendarily dis-tractable Keith Richards of the Rolling Stones managed it. Waking

---

* No? Just me? Never mind . . .

up one morning to find he had recorded the riff to "Satisfaction" on a tape during the night. But it's no coincidence that the Stones's early U.S. tours also took in a lot of musical sightseeing—like pilgrimages to the Chess Records studio in Chicago where so many of their blues heroes recorded, or to L.A. to work with Phil Spector. If you want writing on the road to work for you, you have to make sure you're still being exposed to lots of brilliant music, not just your band's unchanging setlist and the drummer's iPod through the bus speakers for ten weeks solid.

If you have got some interesting songs out of the process you still need to write more now the band is focused and revived. They will, most likely, be far better.

Writing in the Studio

So if you've returned from touring with only some cowboy shirts, an intravenous drug addiction, and an unidentified rash to show for yourself, don't worry. There's no harm in having to write the whole album from scratch. Well, okay, there is a bit of harm. You might end up having to write it in the studio. As writing songs should really be a case of chucking them out and seeing how they go, it's quite a risk for newish bands to try it in that situation. There are too many variables. And studio toys are far too exciting. If a song doesn't work, it's too easy to blame the guitar sound or the drum sound, or ask to use one of the giant echo chambers than to address the far more likely problem—a worthless song. Once you get into all that nonsense, there's a worrying chance that you'll be stuck in the studio forever, chasing your tails and never quite finishing off any songs.

Equally important, all that time will be costing the record company lots and lots of money. So they will, quite fairly, expect a

Figure 14. Second Album Venn Diagram

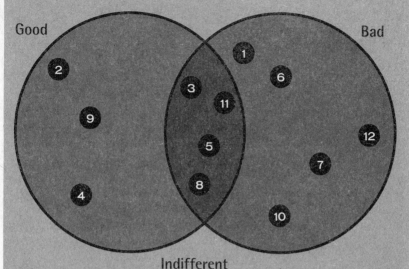

Good

Bad

Indifferent

Key: The Types of Album

1. The same as the first but with fewer hooks and posher drums
2. The same as the first but with slightly better songs
3. A brave departure
4. A backs-against-the-wall triumph
5. A band still in development
6. A desperate bid for fashion
7. A six-producer, twenty-studio cash drain
8. The real musical intentions of the band uncovered after a fashionable debut
9. A gargantuan, over-the-top ballbuster, rammed full of tunes
10. A solid follow-up
11. A crowd-pleaser
12. So distressingly last year

finished album at the end of it. Not a stack of curious demos with potential and a couple of stand out singles. They will cut their losses and release it. But you need to avoid that. You should be aiming to go into the studio with a stack of curious demos with potential and a couple of stand-out singles, not leave with one.

A Stack of Curious Demos with Potential and a Couple of Stand-Out Singles

In fact, that's *exactly* what you should be aiming for when you're writing and rehearsing for album two. Once you've got that, and a producer with some really exciting ideas on how to pull it all together, you are ready to book the studio time and get to work. Then all that recording fun from the last chapter can begin all over again. This time under even more pressure

By the way, if you're one of our Studio Bands from the Heart-Head Horseshoe in chapter 2, you will have recorded three albums worth of material in the time it's taken the others to get over touring and make it to this point. Not that you can be complacent. You need to join them on the next page in assessing just how good your latest venture really is.

How Difficult Is It?

There are, as with so many things band related, only a few types of second album. Some are inherently good, some bad, and some kind of okay. The vast majority hiding their heads under the umbrella of the latter two. So take a listen to what you've got done so far, match it to a category below, and see where it falls on the wonderful Reverend Venn's diagram (*see Fig. 14, p. 181*). Indifferent is fine, as long as you can still remember the songs when you're back home from the studio. If you're in the bad category, though, there's going to be a lot of rerecording ahead. Still, that's better than settling for the alternative—a terrible record that ruins everything you've worked so hard for. A pointless second album is all too frequently bandalism's biggest blow.

The Ten Sure Signs That the Album You're Currently Making Is Shit

But with the pressure on, sometimes it's hard to be detached enough to have that kind of overview. Especially if you're frantically trying to get all the vocals in tune five minutes before the record company comes down to take a listen. So as an extra precaution, for those of you still unsure what kind of an album you're in the middle of creating, on the following pages are ten guaranteed ways to tell if the album you're currently making is shit:

1. Some of the songs have names like "x" song—where x is the track number or key*

> If you can't bother giving it a proper name, why should I bother listening to it?

2. There are songs about being on tour

> Fuck off. Do I make you read my to-do list or watch videos of me at work?

3. You've gone political

> A political conscience is an admirable thing, writing ill-informed songs about political figures just because you've run out of things to say about your

---

* Some bands have gotten away with this. Blur's "Song 2" for example. Or Forward Russia, whose songs are named in the order they were written – "One," "Two," etc. Though the latter haven't made a second album (yet).

private life is not. You are not Woody Guthrie. We all know you only watch the news when the drums are being miked-up and you have nothing better to do.

4. You've been using the phrase "I think the songs on this album are a lot darker" in interviews

What you mean is that they're all meandering dirges because you have forgotten how to write proper choruses. And they're full of minor chords because you've just started learning to play the piano and they sound cooler on it than major ones.

5. You recorded it using a mixing desk that a legendary album was made on

Yeah, that'll work. If I smoke the same cigarettes as David Bowie, it doesn't mean I'll suddenly write "Starman." It's a mixing desk, not Paul fucking Daniels.

6. There's a song about your child

If you love the thing, spend some quality time watching it grow up. Don't waffle on about its miraculous beauty when you're always hiding away in a recording studio or a tour bus when it needs feeding in the middle of the night.

7. Some of the songs mention recording practices

If your life is so empty that you cling to the language of the studio like driftwood on the ocean of confused mediocrity, it's over. Using words like "edit," "erase," and "rewind" is not clever metaphor, but unforgivable

laziness. Stop now and demand to be let out for two
months to live life again.

8. You're writing self-referential lyrics about the band

Yes the Beatles got away with it, when they'd been the
biggest band on earth for five years. You are not. You
are not even the biggest band in New Haven. Hence,
no one cares. It's not the nineties. We all know that
self-referential actually means artistically void.

9. There are songs about the hardships of minor celebrity

Great. Rub it in. See 2:

10. The music's gotten heavier

When is putting on weight a good thing? Music is
like anything else in life—bloated = bad and ugly. Oh
I know it sounds mean, but when did you last begin
a compliment, "Those extra thirty pounds really
suit you . . ."? Okay, look at it this way. If you pile a
hundred cushions on someone it will have a negative
impact on their ability to breathe. The same is true
of a heap of raunchy guitar licks on a song. Go to the
mixing desk. Mute everything but one guitar, vocals,
bass, and drums. Crap? Thought so. Overblown can
easily equal genius, but only if you know why you're
doing it. If it's just because you can, stop, run out of
the studio, and keep running in whatever direction
you're heading until you pass out.

I admit that many briefly popular records have been made by dis-
obeying every one of these rules. But that is a testament to good

marketing not good music. And good marketing costs money. Money this album will have to make back. Unless this album sells lots and lots and lots, marketing it to success will make you far less likely to be able to make another one. Better just concentrating and making it good in the first place. If you want to avoid being destitute at the age of thirty-three, ignore briefly popular and stick to good. Otherwise it's straight to landfill . . .

And Beyond . . .

The more observant among you will have noticed that we are most of the way through the book and have only just finished the second album. This is not because of a sneaky hidden agenda for the follow-up—*Bandalism: The Next Ten Years*. Though actually now I wish I'd thought of that earlier.

No, it's because if you reach this stage properly, you now just repeat the last few sections, from "Touring" onward, until you've run out of music to play. I warned you earlier that the rock 'n' roll life was not for the overly complicated or easily bored. When tired artists talk of getting off the album-tour-album-tour treadmill, they are referring to the endless repetition of this cycle. If that sounds bleak to you, you're either in the wrong career, the wrong band, or at the end of your particular creative path. If that's the case, it's time to turn the page and see what happens when it's time for the band to break up.

With any luck, though, it fills you with boundless joy, and you are now staring into the middle distance, hallucinating the box set and the amazing songs you've not yet written . . . No? Oh well, I was just trying to make it sound beautiful.

So What Have We Learned?

- Eating vol-au-vents could destroy your second album
- Never fire someone till you've found a better replacement
- Mental illness is not cured by bullying
- There aren't enough studio effects in existence to cover up a song about your children

BREAKING UP IS SO VERY HARD TO DO

As Axl Rose reminds us, nothing lasts forever, even cold November rain. And what is true of winter precipitation is also true of four smelly and dysfunctional people in a van who play music with a backbeat for a living.

Of course you don't *have* to break up. You could trudge along happily into your dotage, making money for credit card companies years after your original contemporaries, and even some in your band, have fucked-off, withered away, or died.

More likely, though, you will just run out of something—steam/road/songs/energy/people who are still prepared to buy your records and subsidize your work-shy lifestyle, all of the above—and reach the right point to put away your plectrums, arrange all your old memorabilia in a scrapbook, and buy a pub. Or even the right point to launch a solo career (if there could ever be a right point to do that—but anyway, that's coming up).

Inertia and fear often hold bands together long after they have reached this point. More tragic, other bands are cut down in their prime by stupid problems that could easily have been solved. The purpose of this chapter is to correct this failing, for you at least, and to establish whether your band is still bound for glory or just set on a course for session playing and the job center.

The Healthy Band Checklist

If you've been on the album-tour treadmill a while, or if you're just used to screaming at each other all the time in the name of band unity, it might not be immediately apparent whether that point of no return has been reached. It is all too easy to mistake the stresses and strains of a healthy band's evolution with the meaningless, unremitting misery of one that should have broken up six years ago.

The diagnosis starts with a health-check on the band (*see Fig. 15, p. 191*). If you can honestly put a tick in the YES box for most or all of the ten questions that follow, now is not the right time to stop. So ignore how down you're feeling today and relish the fact you are still a member of this band. If there are fewer ticks, it's time to fix things or give up.

Take a deep breath and remember the first time you played together when it sounded brilliant.

Then remember the most recent time you tried to work on a new song.

Then look at the list:

Figure 15. The Healthy Band Checklist

	yes	no
It still feels more like fun than a regular nine-to-five job.	☐	☐
You still get excited by the new songs you are working on.	☐	☐
You honestly feel that there are exhilarating places you can go as a band.	☐	☐
You still feel like you need each other to make your best music.	☐	☐
You continue to play a couple of tracks from the last-but-one album on tour.	☐	☐
You never settle for second best, even if you know you can get away with it.	☐	☐
You are still exhilarated by the band sound and identity.	☐	☐
You truly believe that your best album is still to come.	☐	☐
Your time together feels like a constant stimulant to your nervous system.	☐	☐
You are more excited about the next album than compiling a B-sides collection.	☐	☐

If you have ticked any of the boxes in the "no" column, your head sinking lower on your chest with an ever-despairing shake and nod of the head, then your time's up. Get to work on a "gone as far as we can go together as a band . . ." press release, cobble together a cash-in greatest hits, and start collecting a few songs for your first, disappointing solo album. It's not bandalism, it's a mercy killing.

But it's unlikely it will have come that far. You will already have become a very awful band by the time you feel that way. If you are just at the beginning of a slide into discontent, you still have a chance to either turn things around for a glorious return to form, or, at worst, retire at the right moment with genius and dignity intact (ensuring a big retrospective in *Rolling Stone* every year and a guaranteed position in the top one hundred albums of all time lists on the TV forever). Which means you'll keep selling records together even if you can't stand looking at each other.

With any luck, though, there'll be a way to return this band to health. And, as with alcoholism and car maintenance, admitting you have a problem is the first step toward averting a disaster.

The Life Cycle of a Band

So is it terminal? On the graph (*see Fig. 16, p. 193*), I have plotted the ideal life cycle of a band. If your answers to the checklist were a bit vague—some positives, some negatives—you have probably hit the Break-Up Zone. If so, you need a bit more of a guide to help you work out whether there is something left to salvage and how to jump on the dotted line back to glory.

Taking a closer look at a small section of the graph known as the Break-Up Zone (*see Fig. 17, p. 194*), I have listed the problems you are probably facing. Some are just blips. You just need to address your issues and snap out of your gloom.

Figure 16. The Life Cycle of a Band

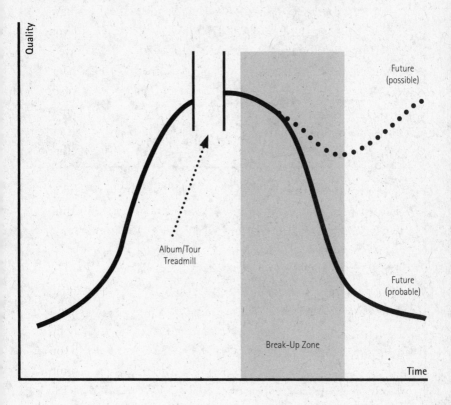

Quality

Future
(possible)

Album/Tour
Treadmill

Future
(probable)

Break-Up Zone

Time

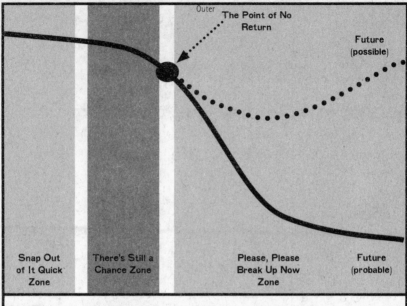

Outer **The Point of No Return**

Future (possible)

Snap Out of It Quick Zone   **There's Still a Chance Zone**   **Please, Please Break Up Now Zone**   **Future (probable)**

Figure 17. The Break-Up Zone (detail)

Snap Out of It Zone

I didn't join a band to . . .

    . . . spend all my time in meetings

    . . . play to people like this

    . . . be broke all the time

    . . . end up living in London/L.A./Outer Space

    . . . to make *you* famous

GO TO P. 195

There's Still a Chance Zone

It feels stagnant	GO TO P. 200 OR P. 214
You hate each other	GO TO P. 200 OR P. 214
You feel like a different person to the one who started in the band	GO TO P. 204
Someone wants to leave	GO TO P. 207
Someone's died	GO TO P. 207
You don't really sell any records anymore	GO TO P. 213
You've been dropped by your label	GO TO P. 213

Please, Please Break Up Now Zone

The magic has gone

You can't agree on any musical common ground

You haven't really got any new ideas

You feel like you've gone as far as you can with this band

GO TO P. 214

If you recognize your band in that first list, it doesn't have to be terminal. Head for the "Snap Out of It" section below.

Others are more troublesome but still don't necessarily mean the end. You have not quite reached "The Point of No Return." For you "There's Still a Chance," so find your ailment in that list and follow the page number next to it to find a suitable solution.

For the rest, those in the "Please, Please Break Up Now" section, it's time to face the unpleasant truth and go to "After the Band Has Gone" on page 214.

Snap Out of It

In the easiest cases, the band is not doomed so much as going through a rough patch. Once a band's ambitions and intentions have been refracted by the real world, it can start to look like a very different beast to the one that formed. When you feel like the band has shifted course or failed to live up to your fantasies, the sentence always begins, "I didn't join a band to . . . " Sometimes that's just a healthy part of moving forwards. More often it leads to a disgruntled member on the phone to his mom in a grim hotel room on the other side of the planet, swigging from a bottle of Jack Daniel's shouting, "I didn't join a band to play fucking trade conferences for arms dealers. I only wanted us to get in the *NME*," before sniffing back the tears and saying, "Mom, I'm coming home."

But such "I didn't join a band to . . . " bandalistic frustrations can usually be eased. So here are a few pragmatic suggestions on how to do that with the most likely complaints:

I Didn't Join a Band to Spend All My Time in Meetings

Once the money has started rolling in, you need sensible grown up people to come in and stop you blowing the lot on smack. On top of the financial price tag, such advice also comes at the cost of having to spend hours and hours in meeting rooms poring through pages of polysyllabic subclauses or mysterious dancing columns of numbers. Somewhere, dimly in the back of your brain, you remember your job is playing guitar in a band. Doing all this properly is very sensible, but it is also dull and distracting.

Even record company meetings about videos, or about approving changes to your MySpace site, are still basically business meetings. Some members are likely to be more interested in these different areas than others. Just leaving them to it and not turning up is fine, but then you forfeit the right to complain if you don't like the decisions they make. Letting those with the strongest interest in the subjects go to the relevant meetings is the simplest solution. If you're in a band with people you don't trust to even buy your cigarettes or use a corkscrew without accidentally blinding themselves, let alone make decisions for the band, you will just have to write off many hours of your own time to the land of humming air conditioning and computers. No, you didn't join a band to spend all your time in meetings, but, unfortunately, you did join one that exists in the real world.

I Didn't Join a Band to Play to People Like This

The lights flare up from the stage and all you can see is a vast ocean of swaying, ugly people. Mainly couples. Ugly couples. How dare they like your band? You're not even an ugly band. You want to be in a cool band that cool people like, not one that would make a Dire Straits audience look like edgy fashionistas.

Well, you aren't, so get over it. If you make music you think is brilliant but the only people who agree are arenas full of grotesque suburbanites, just thank the lord you're popular. If you still care about the music and enjoy it, it's not worth giving up, or even radically changing direction, just for the sake of being a bit more credible. Unless you sold out to get there of course. Then you're really screwed. Time to start looking through job postings . . .

I Didn't Join a Band to Be Broke

When you get recognized in the street it's so someone can shuffle up and tell you how wonderful you are, but no one actually buys your records. You can't even afford an apartment that's big enough to put all your guitars in and you're still having to put your epic meisterworks down on tape in budget demo studios. You love what you do but just can't afford it anymore. Besides, you're thirty-two and everyone else you know has bought a house and gets to go on vacation. If the next album bombs, you're seriously considering retraining as a lawyer.

Cult status is hard. If you leap onto the gleaming chute of commerce you risk getting it wrong or losing all the people who actually do buy your records. You don't *try* not to be popular. You don't see why you're not on the radio all the time. You think you do sound commercial. But sadly the record buying public obeys some other mysterious agenda.

You could always hope for the Flaming Lips option—arriving accidentally at a commercial sound after years of cult appreciation in the middle of your most aggressively uncommercial album,[*] then bring out the glitter balloons and the fluffy animals and some entertaining branding to carve your own individual place in the mainstream. If that doesn't appeal, hold on during the lean times, go and do a quirkily un–rock 'n' roll job for a while[†] and wait for

---

[*] The wonderful *Zaireeka*—one album on four CDs designed to be listened to simultaneously on four different stereos. During the course of making this epic musical statement they also ended up writing most of the songs on their perfect pop career highlight record, *The Soft Bulletin*—which you really ought to own. It's far better than *Yoshimi* . . .

[†] For example, Vic Goddard of Subway Sect, who augmented his musical income by working as a postman.

the box set and accompanying tour. Chuck out a new album a year later and you'll probably have enough cash to get you through a few more years.

The idea of quitting a great band just because it isn't making cash goes against the theme of this book. But sometimes you just feel too old and tired to be plugging away at it. And if you do feel that way, your next record probably won't be all that good, so maybe now is the time to quit. Though the better plan is still to push for the box set.

I Didn't Join a Band to End Up Living in London/L.A./ Outer Space

It's a given in music that a lot of artists like to move to the city where their industry is based. It's more convenient. And for some, the bright lights of showbiz bring out their moth-like tendencies in seconds. Others might be a bit more fond of where they come from and balk at the notion of moving to a place they despise. It's a bit of a disaster if you have one of each in the band.

Bands that lose touch with their roots usually go wrong. But bands that have to travel miles to get to TV studios, record company offices, and the industry at large usually get ignored, so there are strong arguments for both points of view. Being practical, if the majority of the band moves, you will probably have to as well. With any luck, after a couple of years you'll be able to afford more than one place to live and get a house back home too. If you just don't want to leave, or if only one member of the band feels the lure of the big city, then the troublesome one will just have to compromise by putting up with long commutes. Bands don't get to be at home much in their best years anyway, so wherever you live won't make that much difference. Better moving, or traveling, though, than splitting up for the sake of postal codes and geographical prejudice.

I Didn't Join a Band to Make *You* Famous

This old chestnut. Maybe this sentence went through Jam drummer Rick Buckler's mind when security wouldn't let him in the doors at an arena show they were playing on their final tour. Once frontman Paul Weller was in the building, the band's crew seemed relatively untroubled by the lack of a drummer. Status awareness becomes an even more frequent and unwanted visitor the larger a band gets. By the time you're huge it's pretty much a stalker. The closest some members will come to one.

But if you joined a band as a drummer, then, to the public at least, joining a band to make someone else famous is *exactly what you did*. In return for having to deal with less of the hassle. The opposing complaint from the star would be, "I didn't join a band to lose all my privacy and get people interrupting my private conversations to ask for autographs, or what my lyrics mean, every time I go out. I certainly didn't join a band to get photos taken of me looking like crap every time I go to the shop for some milk."

The negative aspects of fame are balanced fairly evenly across all members of a band. As long as the famous ones don't go all rock star* and the rest don't get bitter and self-pitying, it really isn't a problem. Besides, if you are a C type personality (our Quiet Ones, Moody Ones, and Enthusiastic Amateurs from the quiz in chapter 1) and you'd got to be frontman, the band would never have gotten anywhere in the first place.

---

* "Get back in goal, goalie," as Noddy Holder's character sneers at drummer Don Powell's in *Slade in Flame*, when the latter attempts to get involved in a band dispute.

There's Still a Chance

These are the more involved problems and take more concerted working out. But even if one of these greater perils is threatening the band, there may still be a joyous way forward.

How to Survive . . . Reinvention

The magic may not have disappeared entirely, but the conjuror is certainly putting away his string of knotted hankies and looking for his car keys. If you still pretty much get along and like the idea of the band, but haven't written a decent song for six albums, it could be time for a drastic rethink.

Change for the sake of it is usually a very worrying sign in bands. Suddenly switching from mild pop/rock to beat-splitting dance rock could smack of desperation and alienate your entire existing fanbase (no one likes to see a band panicking). But this is not change for the sake of it. This is now change to survive. You might be clinging to a certain sound or a certain way of writing songs simply because it's what you're used to. You are a band, not an Edwardian grocers shop, clinging to tradition is not your best business model. And slipping into a fixed routine is not the greatest way to break down the boundaries or pop music, or even to write a ear-tickling chorus.

It's time to look at the music—what music you're into now, what music you really wish you were making—and work from there. Sit down together and play each other the best records you have gotten into in the last year. You are likely to notice any of the following straight away:

1. You all like wildly conflicting things
2. You all like similar things but they sound nothing like your band

3. You have no new records to play each other because none of you listen to new music any more

If it's point 1, there's very little you can do. It's impossible to make the band function if you don't believe in any common musical ground any more. Head straight to page 214.

If it's point 2, then it's time to throw yourselves into a new direction. It may be an embarrassing failure but it's worth the risk. You will be carrying on for a legitimate reason—you all believe there is still great music left to make.

If it's point 3, you need to turn on the radio, go out to gigs and get down to the record shops—you've gotten stale. If you can't be bothered to rekindle your love of music but just stumble into making another record, I will personally come down to the studio, under the cloak of night, and set fire to it.* Whether you're in there or not. Do you really think your favorite records were made by people who didn't give a flying fuck about music? Your own good ones certainly weren't. It's not exactly taxing—I'm asking you to read the reviews section of the paper once in a while, not build a fully functioning power station out of Legos.

And what about if some of your number object to the prospect of such daring novelty? Well, they will have to think very seriously about why they're still in a band. If it's just to play the hits, they can go and join a tribute band.† If they want to make great music still they must accept that that goes hand in hand with novelty and risk. After all, when you first started, no one knew how it would

---

* Thinking about it, that's exactly what fate did to Doves. Still in their previous guise as Sub Sub, the gutting of their studio and necessary subsequent period of taking stock led to their return as the expansive, grumpy indie rockers we all know and love.

† One time Status Quo rhythm section Alan Lancaster and John Coghlan have both occasionally played with Quo tribute bands. Rick Buckler and Bruce Foxton of the Jam have formed their own Jam tribute band.

sound or whether it would work. That's what made the first record so exciting. There was nothing to lose. The fact you have gotten it right before in those circumstances should encourage you this time around rather than scare you off. As my dad said to me once when I was being fussy about trying pizza as a child, "You had to try chips for the first time once."* If you really break out in a rash every time you aren't playing heads-down rock 'n' roll, you're no use to anyone and really shouldn't be in bands any more.

As an extra tip, don't film the experience, however much it seems like a good idea. Both the Beatles (*Let It Be*) and Metallica (*Some Kind of Monster*) tried bringing in the booms and the cameras while they were staggering about searching for a new direction, in each instance a back to basics live band approach. The results are, in both cases, compelling viewing—toe-curlingly hilarious portraits of the bitchy and high-maintenance world of a successful band in turmoil. But neither strike you as particularly happy experiences for the band in question. Living hell would be a more accurate description. Perhaps early camera skeptics were right—maybe film really does steal the soul. It certainly seemed to sap both bands' abilities to concentrate on writing decent songs.

Band Identity

It might still be the same members, you might still be playing the same instruments, the bass player might still be wearing the same pair of trousers he did on the cover of the first album ten years ago, but somehow you just don't feel like a band anymore.

The problem could be that you've moved on as people and your lives have changed. In which case, you need to skip on a couple

---

* In mid-eighties Leicester, pizza seemed like a daring novelty. He was quite right by the way, pizzas ended up eclipsing chips as my favorite food. It's a wonder I'm thin, really—goodness knows what's going to happen once I hit thirty. Anyway, I digress.

of pages to "Growing Apart." But it could just be that somewhere in the haze of itineraries, you have forgotten that you're actually a band—a gang. It might sound superficial, indeed it *is* superficial, but the answer is to go shopping. If dressing like a band and feeling like you're part of a gang make such a big difference when you're starting out, there's no reason for that not to be true once you've sold a few records and put on some weight.

Bands that outlast their contemporaries are usually just as fond of using a judicious trip to Marks & Spencer to keep the flame alive as they are of changing producers and experimenting with new directions.* Just look at the Rolling Stones and their switch to wearing flouncy pajamas around *Exile on Main Street* or fluorescent, skin-tight pseudo sportswear for their 1982 world tour.† Or U2—okay their image changes usually involve slimming black things for Bono and a bald-disguising hat for the Edge, but other than that, they remain relatively flexible.

So if, for you, thinking about image these days consists of running into the Levis shop and picking up some 32/32 507s without even trying them on, you could be ignoring a very potent source for restoring band unity and drive. The key is, whatever point in your career you have reached, bands that feel more unified find it easier to stay together and make good records.

If you're stuck for ideas on how to do it, go back to the image section in chapter 2. Though it's also important, now that you've reached this stage, that you don't alienate your existing audience too much either. Mind you, fans are pretty tolerant creatures. You

---

* If you think I'm joking about my choice of shop, remember that three quarters of the Smiths prepared for their first, legendary, appearance on *Top of the Pops* by nipping in there and buying matching crew-neck jumpers. And they looked great in them. Well, Johnny Marr did anyway.
† A terrible look, granted but it did roughly coincide with their last great single, "Start Me Up." Since then it's just been patchy lifestyle music for aging babyboomers with clothes to match.

have to do something *really* awful for that to happen.[*] And it's always better to challenge your fans a bit for the sake of moving on than just disappoint them incrementally with each release for a trying decade of artistic stasis, until even they get bored of loyalty buying.

How to Survive . . . Growing Apart

It's a Tuesday evening in March. Steve, the singer, is having a dinner party at his new house in Primrose Hill. The guests are a mixture of rising stars of the arts world and a couple of music industry professionals. Corks pop, glasses twinkle, and a homely glow of success envelops the room with a sense of unstoppable confidence. Conversation turns through each other's recent projects to pressing humanitarian questions in the developing world and action on climate change. Sitting next to his beautiful partner though, our band member is a little subdued, privately turning over a graver thought, "I'm sick of Dave."

A few streets down the hill, Dave is sprawled under a dirty duvet on the floor of an unlit room above a dodgy looking 7-Eleven. Full to the gunwales with crack, only dimly aware of his own tawdry existence, with a vague sensation of a thought dully knocking into the back of his skull as it swishes about around his head and up and down his spinal column, "Steve's turned into a right posh twat."

Take a group of people in their early twenties and fling them through the spin-cycle of success, failure, breakdown, triumph,

---

[*] Like Rod Stewart when he started wearing sailor suits and eyeliner in 1975. The Stones actually almost got away with that look the year before, though only for one single. And Mick Taylor did leave straight afterward. Come to think of it, the Manics used it too in about 1993—maybe that's why Richey James Edwards decided to disappear.

pressure, sex, drugs, rock 'n' roll, and truck stops for five years. The people who emerge at the other end are likely to be very different to the ones that went in. Bands are made up of individuals and individuals change.

A band is a social entity and social factors can just as easily drive a big fat spike through it as musical differences. If the rest of the band is a social embarrassment, or just not the sort of people you like hanging about with anymore, collective drive will evaporate and you will start to feel trapped.

So what can you do? If it isn't affecting the quality of the music or the way you work together then you don't have a problem. You can just accept that things are different now. You're older. You don't have to be the same kind of gang anymore.

But, let's be honest, that's very unlikely. Your perceptions of other members of the band are inherently linked to how you interact together musically. If you don't take the rest of the band seriously outside the studio, it's not suddenly going to happen just because you're in a darkened room with a sofa and a water-cooler.

If you don't want to split up and still think there is some good in the band, you'll just have to learn to live with who you all are now. Try to see the positive sides. The different angles you are now approaching the music from could skew the sound in an interesting way. Oh, who am I trying to fool? If you don't have anything in common anymore and you're not grown up enough to just deal with it or accept it and try to find a way of making it work, just go to page 214.

Unfortunately, it's unlikely to be even that straightforward—that everyone in the band hates the way that everyone else in the band has changed. It's more likely that growing apart will be an individual problem—that individual members will feel like they have outgrown their specific roles in the band while others are still happy with them.

Seeing as I've already stuck you in limited personality type categories in this book, it might seem a bit rich to start talking about how damaging that can be. But when people get frustrated by their role, they stop putting their whole soul into the band. And if that happens, the music is likely to get a bit stale. Yes, this will be far more of a problem for the more cerebral band members than the brawnily visceral. But it only needs one member to feel like they have outgrown their role to ruin the whole band.

Not exactly a byword for edgy rock 'n' roll, but the Spice Girls illustrate this point rather well. Once *Top of the Pops Magazine* had branded them with their nicknames (Posh, Sporty, Ginger, etc.) they had individual identities that clicked with the public and they started selling lots of records. But they also had to live those identities. When you look at what's happened to the various members over the last decade, it could be read as five people attempting to come to terms with having had the whole planet sum them up with one word adjectives. Most people like to think they're complicated and can change, so if you're stuck in one very limited role it can feel very frustrating. But in a lot of bands this frustrating limitation is *precisely what makes them good*.

Finding a solution is therefore a challenge. If the bass player starts getting to put instrumental lounge funk workouts in the middle of your albums just to help them feel more valued, self-expressive artistic growth is going way too far. But if they aren't allowed to, they will get bored and want to leave. Which will be just as damaging to the band.

Much like the problems of leadership in the last chapter, the ultimate barometer should always be the quality of the music you're putting out as a result. So if the keyboard player's songs are crap, you will have to find a very subtle way of metaphorically slamming the piano lid down on her fingers. And that's hard to do without alienating someone forever.

So what can you do if a member is discontented with their individual role? Well the quickest and easiest way is to encourage them to make a solo album. Because their songs are so good and deserve an outlet all of their own. Obviously. They would be better put in the spotlights, not buried under that shadows of other band songs. Then just hope they believe you.

The resulting album will be hideous and you will probably have to guest on it. But it will be buried at the bottom of the bargain bin before anyone realizes it's out, and with the accompanying beating to their ego, all their future desire to butcher your band releases with their sub-Enya lift music will hopefully be buried too. Yes they need space to develop as people. But not if that's going to make your records shit. The solo album is by far the best solution to walking this ego tightrope.

How to Survive . . . Losing a Member

There are two ways you lose a band member without firing them— they leave or they die. Both are devastating (especially the latter). And both will accelerate your journey to the point of breaking up before you might otherwise have reached it. From the firing section of the last chapter, you already know how crucial it is not to mess about with the basic make up of a band.

If it's the band's decision, as it is when you fire someone, you can at least control it, or do something to stop it happening. But if someone dies or disappears, there's nothing you can do but try to cope with it. At least if a member is just unhappy and wants to leave there are still a few things you can try.

The main, and frequently overlooked, one is to ask them why they want to go. Sadly, in the real world, more often bands will instead just grunt a sullen "fair 'nuff" at the departing member and let a crucial fraction of their magic disappear. Or launch a big screaming rant at them (Yeah, because *that'll* make them want to stick around). Asking them what's wrong, on the other hand, might get you into a conversation where you can change their mind. It might even reveal a few mystical secrets about why the band is going wrong too.

And what will they say?

"I'm Exhausted"

They need to repair themselves. They need some of the pressure taking off them. But don't just say cool and hire a stand-in. The original member will never come back and you'll be lumbered forever with a stop-gap. If you're all on hold and waiting for them, it might, with any luck, guilt the unhappy member into getting back to normal quicker. But don't let them know you're thinking that. Act like they can take all the time in the world. Do the whole sneaky getting involved in other projects thing and wait for them to get scared and come back.

"Nobody Loves Me Anymore"

Beatles story again—Ringo left for this reason during sessions for *The Beatles* album. He told John Lennon it was because he felt the others were all really close and he was out on a limb. John's response was, "I thought it was you three."* See this is why asking what the problem is can be so important. They could have lost Ringo for no

---

* Ringo was welcomed back into the fold by George Harrison filling the studio at Abbey Road with flowers. Ah!

good reason. If you just spend five minutes making someone feel better you could save the whole band.*

"I Hate This Band"

Well they didn't to start with so what's changed? What do they hate? My guess is it will be covered somewhere in this section, or the "Snap Out of It" one a few pages back. Listen to them. What's making them hate the band might be exactly the same reason why no one's buying your records anymore.

"I Don't Want to Be in a Band Anymore"

Then you're stuck. Explain to them how much the band needs them—how important what they do is to what makes it great. If that still doesn't convince them to stay then you'll have to let them go. We'll come to what you need to do next in a minute.

"I Hate You or I Hate That You All Hate Each Other"

A feud. If this is about a bitter personality battle, you're also in trouble. Even if the music's still sometimes amazing, it's never much fun living under conditions of perpetual hostility, so you can't really blame them. Even members not directly involved in a feud usually get caught up in the crossfire. If it's become too much for them to cope with, you probably won't even be getting the occasional musical benefits of a bad atmosphere. Let them go if the feuding can't be solved. And if they go, is there much point carrying the rest of the band on? Face it, your stupid fighting has fucked the whole thing up.

---

* When George left the next year it was just with the parting salvo, "See you round the clubs." No one bothered asking why and it proved far more time-consuming getting him to come back. Ultimately that was the point when the band finally started to unravel.

"I Don't Think This Band Has a Future"

You might not agree. You might in fact be deluding yourself because you don't want to face the truth. But someone might want to leave the band if they think it is long past its creative prime and has no way of getting back. You could try and prove them wrong, but you might be better off listening very carefully to them to see if what they say is actually true. If it is, it's off to page 214 with you.

So if you've definitely lost someone, what do you do next? Well before you panic and start trying to train your fourteen-year-old brother on the guitar, you have to stop and question whether you *really* want to carry on. Is there anything to be gained from it or will it just not be the same? If a member has died, forget all the "It's what he would have wanted" crap. That's your bank balance talking. Much like "We owe it to the fans to do another record." Like hell you do! You owe it to the building society or the record company and you want the poor old fans to pay for it.

It depends how far through the band life cycle you think you've gotten. If you're a young band with ideas left in you, it might be worth carrying on. The Manic Street Preachers made it work after Richey Edwards's disappearance by reinventing themselves as a different sort of band—one that sold lots of records. Crucially, though, they never tried to *replace* Richey. The Who did when Keith Moon died in 1978 and also tried to press on as if nothing had happened, drafting in old friend Kenney Jones to play the drums. That didn't work at all. Led Zeppelin, faced with the same situation when their own drummer, John Bonham, died two years later, had the dignity to end it there.

And that's the crucial point. Never pretend it hasn't happened. Whether someone leaves, or someone dies, the band left behind is a *different* band. If you want to carry on, go back and reinvent the band for the new circumstances.* Don't think you can just replace someone and carry on as before. The point of bands is that members can't actually be replaced—bands are about unique combinations of individuals. That's why some are brilliant when on paper they shouldn't be and some terrible when they should. You can find someone new and possibly be just as good, but you can never be the same.

So if you are going to recruit a new member, don't just look for a budget replicant of the departed one. You have to go right back to finding a member from chapter 1 and only pick someone that fits one of the three criteria (You Like Them, You Like Something About Them, You Like Something About Playing with Them, and NOT You Like the Fact They're a Bit Like the Last Person You Had), see what they bring to the band and start again.

Just as important, don't carry on for the sake of it. If the band was already looking quite sick when the person went, or if they left because they were jumping from a sinking ship, then it's time to move on to page 214.

How to Survive . . . Growing Up

In Metallica's *Some Kind of Monster*, which dramatizes the quandaries of this chapter with painful unintended hilarity, there is a scene in which singer James Hetfield tries to sing a guide vocal to a song in the studio while bouncing his child on his knee. His guttural, nihilistic ranting seems a trifle incongruous as he gently rocks his offspring. Drummer Lars Ulrich too displays a mixture of glowing pride and slight annoyance when, in a later scene, he watches his son thrash around on his drum kit.

---

* As Joy Division did when singer Ian Curtis died. Their reinvention from atmospheric gloom to dead-pan dance pop was convincing enough to make New Order a far more popular band of the time.

Being in a band may well seem to give you free reign to behave like a teenager in perpetuity. But however staunchly one tries to stay young, dumb, and irresponsible, real life has a nasty habit of tripping you up eventually, changing your priorities and circumstances. What started as your ticket to escape, becomes, on arriving at the destination of success, a big unwieldy placard around your neck impeding your ability to settle down and live a nice comfortable life.

This realization, more than any other moment, is the Point of No Return. Being in a band, and making music in general, is resistant to compromize. The emotion you put into the music is all too easy to decipher for the astute listener at the other end. If it felt edgy, it sounds edgy. If it felt panicked and desperate, sadly it sounds that way too. And if it felt half-hearted, well by Jove, that's just how it will sound to all but the most cloth-eared member of the public. Hence why no one listens to the big fanfare releases of established bands anywhere near as often as they do their earlier records. Or at least no one with any sort of taste or discernment.

Wouldn't it be lovely if you could balance being in a band at its creative peak with being a normal human being? But you can't. For the songwriters at least, music has to be an unregulatable passion.[*] If you try to fit it in alongside picking the kids up from school it will show. It will become music to fill the diary rather than music to fill the soul.

If you want the band to continue and be any good, you will *all* have to devote unhindered time to it. Maybe not all year, but

---

[*] Like Freddie Mercury, who slept with a piano as the headboard of his bed so he could work out songs in the middle of the night without having to get up. He even taught himself to play piano upside down behind his head so he could stay lying down.

certainly for months on end, especially when engaged in the creative part. This is possible, but it's hard. But sadly this is the choice—making huge sacrifices or breaking the band up now. Only your hearts and your wallets can answer this one for you.

How to Survive . . . Failure

Finding the right time to break up is not only the band's decision. Sometimes other people pass you helpful hints—like the record company dropping you or no one turning up to your gigs any more. Negative enlightenment, if you will. If loads of people seem to be telling you you've lost it, it's, at the very least, a wise precaution to have a bit of a check and see if they're right.

There are more reasons than just music that sink a band's career. Fashion, timing, bad luck, and other bands copying your ideas and getting more famous from it can all play a part. But if your Healthy Band Checklist looks a bit sketchy *and* you aren't even filling pubs five years after you used to pack stadiums, something's going a bit awry.

If you still have the will to carry on, you need to try and look for the point when it all went wrong. The disastrous concept album about bees? The desperate grope toward contemporary fashion because you didn't think you were cool enough? Then you need to ask some questions. Do you still want to make the sort of music that made you popular? And would that sort of music still make you popular again now? If not, have you got any ideas for reinventing yourselves? Could you do it well or would it just be forced? Or are you just sick of all this band shit anyway? If you've got to the last question, it's time to move on to the next section.

After the Band Has Gone

Before you decide to stick your instruments on eBay and delete the drummer's number from your phone, it's time for one final reality check. A reality check in its most literal sense—you need to remind yourself what reality actually is and have a bit of a think about whether returning to it is such a good idea.

Big, heavy band conversations that sprawl out of control into bitter, confused fights are not very nice. But they are nicer than stacking shelves in a supermarket and trying to work out what jobs are available to twenty-nine-year old former musicians with GEDs and no transferable skills.

Right now you might not be so sure—exhausted and ravaged after five years on the album-tour waltzers. But, trust me, being a pop star, even an unhappy one, is still better. You coped with depressing jobs before you were successful, but then you were going somewhere and confident. And you hadn't got used to being surrounded by a support team of people whose job it is to make sure you don't run out of toilet paper (well, apart from your parents). The real world is horrible. That's why you tried so hard to escape from it. If you're thinking of going back to it, you need to remember exactly what that will involve.

And here's how you do it. Go through all of your non-music industry friends in your head (if you have any left) and think of the one who has the most depressing job. It might be squalid, it might be well-paid but soul-sapping—"depressing" is after all a fairly subjective term—but there must be someone who always makes you think, "How the hell do they actually get up in the morning?" Ring them up and ask if you can shadow them at work for a week. You'll have to lie about the reason—say it's research for a concept album or a film or something. When you get back home again at the end of the week, ask yourself if you're still sure about breaking up the band. Then get really drunk.

Does It Have to Be so Depressing?

No. This is just shock tactics. My simplistic attempts at manipulation. The future may not look as bleak as all that. I just want you to have a bit of perspective before you take out the big bandalism mallet and break up on a stupid whim you'll later regret.

And I'm duty bound to present the alternative outcome: there are also good things that could happen if you break up the band. The future may be just as glorious and dazzling for you as the last few years have been. You might be able to stick around in the unreal world of music. That's if being in a band hasn't put you off forever.

So to see if there's a future for you in rock 'n' roll, it's time for me to put on my careers guidance hat and show you what that future looks like. And more specifically, what it might hold for each of our ten band member personality types.

A—The Natural Leader

Life for you doesn't look too frightening. The most likely next step would be a solo career. But it's worth taking a couple of seconds to remember again just how bad they normally are. And that you will be forever singing over the echoes of your former band. If you have no problems with playing mediocre covers of that band's old greatest hits with bored session musicians then this might be quite painless*. Being something of a pragmatist,

---

* Maybe ask Richard Ashcroft about it after another gig to a restless audience itching to hear "Bittersweet Symphony" or "The Drugs Don't Work" and going for a wee or talking during the new stuff. Since writing this book, the Verve reformed. This might be the answer . . .

you might also enjoy not having to split the money equally at the end. Also in this option's favor, it pays the bills, you still get cheered at lots, and you don't need to retrain.

If you can't stomach that, you could always form another band. When Free ceased to exist, singer Paul Rodgers took drummer Simon Kirke with him to form Bad Company. Learning from Free's mistakes, they finally conquered America with their brand of safe, plodding blues-rock. Much as the Small Faces' Steve Marriott did with his follow-up band, Humble Pie. So while your next step could be pleasingly lucrative, but you must accept that it's also very unlikely to change the world.

B–The Artist

You've got the talent, you've usually got the songs, but as we know, you're sometimes a bit lacking on the common sense. You might also try a solo career, but for you that could also be a shorthand for spending ten years locked in your home studio, burning up royalties on old microphones and mixing desks, and never actually managing to finish off a song, let alone release it. Unchecked by the rest of the band, it could also mean records that redefine the word "patchy" with ill-advised genre shifts and ludicrous pretension.

If you form another band, it will either be full of hapless yesmen and your pointless noodling, or unbelievably, it could be genuinely intriguing and experimental. Even good. The latter though only if you allow yourself proper collaboration and treat it like a proper band. Even then it will still be fearsomely misguided at times. And it goes without saying that you'll refuse to play any old songs and be confused about why that annoys your fans so much. You'll also be constantly jealous that you don't make as much money as the singer is doing now.

C—The Quiet One

Sometimes Quiet Ones form new bands. Sometimes they even fight their fear of the limelight and try to go solo. You shouldn't. It will be ghastly, journeyman stuff—like the Natural Leader's second band but without the slick showbiz. Like a band of bass players, in fact.

So what can you do? A bit of session work perhaps? But you like a bit of certainty, so if you take that option, it won't be long before you end up joining another band permanently. And my money's on one of your old rivals. Your future could easily involve playing someone else's greatest hits and being constantly misidentified in pictures as the person you replaced.

Far better to leap into the swivel chair and start fiddling with faders. Your behind-the-scenes geekery and unflappable nature might make you an excellent record producer. Certainly a safe, solid, and reliable one. And they're the ones that get the most regular work. There are as yet unmade middle-of-the-road chart hits just waiting to swamp your bank account. Ah—the glamour of Pro Tools edit screens! It could all be yours!

D—The Lairy-Mad-for-It Lunatic

Question? (as Beyoncé might put it). Why the fuck do you want to stay in music? You were barely involved with it to start with. What on earth do you think you're going to do? Like the Quiet One you could always join one of your old rivals/contemporaries—as a Lairy-Mad-for-It Lunatic for hire, giving them a shot in the arm of purest rock 'n' roll.

In fact, try and do that. The other alternatives aren't so promising. Short-lived management of wildly unmarketable bands (whose slim chances of success you render non-existent through your own unquenchable thirst for irresponsibility). Session work is largely out too. Unless people want your very specific sound and are prepared to spend six days and four broken microphones on the privilege. As for a solo career—dear God, no! Instead get someone to ghost-write your memoirs and spend your days holding court in your local bar in return for free drinks.

A+B—The Hustler

Session-playing gun for hire and all round self-promotion machine I reckon. You're well-connected and a self-proclaimed genius so you will hardly be lacking offers. You're also a good talker. Maybe you could even get yourself on the radio or the TV talking about music. That way you'll still stay famous. A solo career or a new band will probably end up in the (exceptionally) gray area between the Natural Leader and the Artist.

Management's certainly an option, creating a bit of buzz being instinctive for you. Whether you will be such a good talent spotter is another matter. You'll probably only want to work with bands that are trying to be a worse version of you and even then you'll end up ripping them off somewhere along the way. Well if they don't want to be exploited, they shouldn't be in rock 'n' roll should they?

A+C—The Backseat Driver

If you form another band, there's a high chance it will be pretty good. Very successful even. Though tainted with a slight streak of cash-grabbing, cold-blooded opportunistic cynicism.

But why would you want to do that when there are new people to cajole and bully from the background? Other bands to manage perhaps. Or produce. Or even, more fittingly for your brand of subtle manipulation, to sign to record labels. You have been unofficial internal A&R policeman for your band all these years, you'll probably take great delight in doing the same thing officially, and getting rewarded properly for it. You could find a great band, make decisions for them and boss them about a bit. Yay.

Whichever path you pick, you'll be extra-sure of your convictions thanks to the unassailable cool of your rock 'n' roll credentials. You could take over the world! Again.

A+D—The Cool One

Who are you trying to fool? You don't want to stay in music. You might do the odd celebrity collaboration, but you won't be sitting up till 2:00 a.m. worrying about where to go next—other than worrying about which invitation to a rarefied social function you feel like accepting. There will be no tortured solo album. No backs-against-the-wall starting a new band and conquering the world. There will just be interesting offers, unusual projects, and a certain amount of laurel-resting until you accidentally get a novel published, or put money into a really successful restaurant or go into rehab and come out the other side as a well-reputed sculptor.

B+C—The Moody One

Something tells me that you won't be too desperate to go through this band stuff all over again. Not with a whole new bunch of people. A solo career might work though. Imagine making records the way you want them rather than having to have them fucked about with by a bunch of squabbling half-wits. For this reason, where you go next might bring out a lot of your C type personality leanings—i.e., it will be very conservative stuff. You'll also be so picky about it all that the records will sound scouring-pad clean. Which could of course mean that you sell loads and loads of them. Mainly to older people. Older men. Alan Partridge.

You might not be too bad in the producer's chair. You would certainly exact tough quality control standards from your charges. For them the sessions will probably be an unending torrent of insensitive nit-picking and brutal sarcasm. But they'll get the hits. At some point you will also get really stroppy that no one talks about you as much as the rest of the band and disappear from music in a huff for a while to become a farmer.

B+D—The Self-Destructive Genius

Well, let's start with the positive angle. Off-the-wall, challenging, brilliant-but-flawed solo albums could keep you going for a lifetime. Though no doubt separated by increasingly long gaps between releases and quality control that slackens from crap to nonexistent. That's assuming you're still together enough at this stage to remember how to hold a plectrum. Your records will appear to a fanfare of critical praise and career retrospectives then disappear again rapidly when you pull out of tours or play bad gigs wearing silly things. Then there will be the wilderness years—no doubt including a baffling dabble with free jazz or body-activated synthesizers, or even a spell in prison—then the unexpected return, more commercial disaster, and another long, messed-up hiatus.

You can forget about sideways jumps into the industry side. And session playing is out—you're only really any good at playing your songs. In the old days you might have moved into production and made fabulously weird records with obscure bands. But it would be a brave label now that put you in the studio with a new band and any kind of commercial intentions. And a very scared one that turned up after a week of sessions to find only one track recorded—a studio jam of "Get Back" played on a coat-hanger and a pack of cirgarettes.

C+D—The Enthusiastic Amateur

Well, there's the tribute band option I mentioned earlier. Erm . . . there aren't all that many choices for you really. It's probably most realistic to look at a future that doesn't involve you bashing your kit or strumming your rhythm guitar. If you get session work, it will be based on your old band and will probably dry up when people forget who you are or realize you're not actually that amazing a player. Production then? Maybe, but the same rules largely apply unless it's a style of music your really enjoy. A new band? A solo career? I'm not sure you'd know where to start. You never wrote the band's songs and you certainly weren't the sex symbol. If you've made enough cash, just potter about and enjoy your hobbies. Even if you haven't, just do this on a budget. What about after-dinner speaking?

So Is It Finally Time?

Now you know what's coming, you can make a proper decision on whether to break up the band. And if you've used up all your creative juice it's probably the best, and certainly the coolest, decision to take. Break up a band before you get too bad and you can jump around merrily on the springy mattress of reputation for the rest of your earthly days. Think of all those lives you have enriched and stride off into the sunset. With an optional guitar slung nonchalantly over your shoulder for a suitably Hollywood silhouette . . .

. . . unless you decide just to put the band on hold for a bit instead. And I warn you, that sounds like a bit of a cop out to me. If there is still the spirit in the band to carry it on at some unspecified point in the future, then there is nothing inherently wrong with disappearing off for a couple of years to work on extra-curricular projects or recuperate. If someone's gone a bit mad or if members have itchy feet that might be a way around the problem.

But it's a risk. The problem with a sabbatical is that when you return, your magic will have evaporated and you will have grown too used to working separately to enjoy collaboration. Leading to squabbling, half-assed compromise, and all the other rubbish things we've now come across several thousand times. Though if it's a choice between this and definitely breaking up at least it's a good natured way of doing it that reduces the likelihood of your fans coming round and trying to kill you. Let's be honest though, it's breaking up for cowards.

It Ain't Over Till You're All Dead

"Dave. I've just had Harvey Goldsmith on the phone. A hundred grand a night each for a twenty-date arena tour. A hundred fifty if they choose the setlist. What do you reckon? I kind of said yeah anyway. I mean obviously . . . without . . . well you know since Rob's . . . gone . . . we'll have to get someone else in and stuff. But seriously, man—I think it's the right time. And I know Rob'd have told us, 'do it,' y'know . . ."

Should you ever reform?

Is it ever the right thing to do?

No.

Yes you might get back in the room, looking over your instruments at your older, jowlier selves—guitars at a height for comfort over cool, graying roadies placing your four hundred effects pedal unit down in the exact right spot, Harley Street throat specialist's mobile number at the ready, a sea of tasteful leisure slacks and unfeasibly expensive custom built amplifiers—and you'll grin at each other. You've still got that spark. It's still there. It's like you only split up last week.

"Shit! That sounded amazing! I think we're better now than we were twenty years ago."

Of course you think that, you deluded twat. You've just played one of your old songs. They're amazing compared to rambling musical cotton wool you've been spewing out since you were thirty. You've just been potently reminded of what it was like when you were young and talented. That's bound to make you feel pretty good.

Actually, though, it sounded like horribly overprocessed guitars, woefully out-of-time drums, a completely different bass line and a singer whose voice now sags around the notes like over-stocked shelves heaving under aging canned goods in a particularly shabby old corner shop.

"The new bass line's really cool, Mike."

"Yeah. I didn't know *anything* back then."*

And that's just at your first rehearsal playing your best-known song. God help us when you get back from the wallet-bulging, stress-free nostalgia fest of a tour and decide you've got some NEW MATE-RIAL. There are two likely consequences:

1. You get into the studio and after a day and a half, all the jovial old-soldier camaraderie dissipates. Guards drop, tempers fray, and hissy fits erupt into screaming threats regarding unfinished legal cases. It *really* is like you only broke up last week—in that you get a

---

* Not that I'm making a comparison, but Dave Gilmour described the reforming of Pink Floyd at Live 8 as being "like sleeping with your ex-wife." Curmudgeonly, perhaps, but refreshingly unsentimental.

powerful instantaneous reminder of why you all started hating each other so much in the first place. The project is quietly shelved. Or even worse shudders to its conclusion—a milk-curdling approximation of your old sound with a lead single so bad that it disappears off the radio after its first excruciating, excremental exclusive play. A nation looks at its shoes muttering, "That's not it. That's not it at all" under its breath.

2. Well-drilled, over-produced soft rock of the kind that any random combination of session musicians would jam as a default if they were left alone with their instruments for twenty minutes. Accompanied by lyrics of such crass banality and overblown self importance that the long past his prime singer sounds like God reading aloud from a packet of Lovehearts— yelping, "The world ain't such a bad place, darlin'" six-notes above his trussed-in leather-trousered range.

And don't think that just because you're only in your early thirties it won't be quite as hideous. Reforming is bad. But until every original member of the band is dead it is a perpetual threat.*

Okay there are some exceptions. Reforming to play a one-off gig or tour for money-grabbing and desperate reasons is at least quite fun for the fans as long as it goes no further.† Or there is the band that genuinely has some unfinished business. If after a couple of

---

* Even the death of a singer is no guarantee against terrible new material. Queen and the Beatles made that abundantly clear in the nineties—"It's what he would have wanted" taken to a gruesome extreme as they rifled through old demos to make new money. Actually, I quite like "Free as a Bird." But the point still stands. And "Real Love" is shit.

† Roxy Music at Wembley in 2001 was fantastic.

years you just have to work together again to make the sort of music you want to make, maybe reforming can be justified. Like when the Verve reformed in 1997 and finally sold shitloads of records with *Urban Hymns*. But then if the Verve had followed this chapter, they would never have split up in the first place.

So what about their one time label-mates Embrace then? Rescued from the bin and replaced on the out-of-tune anthemic mantelpiece by a song that Chris Martin didn't deem good enough for his own band. It was certainly a good financial decision. It opened them up to a far bigger audience than they ever had before. But do you ever really find yourself waking up in the morning thinking, "I'm so fucking glad that Embrace are with us again?" With reforming there is only the okay, the terrible, and the absolutely unforgivable.

So here is a guideline—every horrible note you play as a re-formed band erases the work done by five good ones the first time around. Ten if the new note's played in a new song. If you don't mind this systematic wiping of your back catalog's credibility then go ahead. Reforming can after all be lucrative. But then so are fraud and international drug trafficking. If you put the band in the past for good reasons then leave it there. You might sometimes reminisce about how great your schooldays were too, but you don't dig out a pair of ill-fitting shorts and start hanging around in playgrounds. You'd get arrested.

The past is a foreign country, they do things differently there. In your case the difference being that you used to have hunger, good ideas, and the superhuman confidence of four or five people certain they were going to make the world a better place with brilliant records. Now you have a gut, a big kitchen with an Aga, and your parasite children sell their wedding pictures to *Hello*. Your visa to get to the past has long since expired. In fact, you're on a blacklist.

If you miss the old days, go for a drink with the bass player and stay up till three listening to old demos. Or shove out a box set and buy a holiday home on the proceeds. Just leave the fucking band alone.

So What Have We Learned?

- Having ugly fans is not a legitimate reason to break up a band
- Finding a new drummer when the last one's just died is not "what he would have wanted" unless he hated you
- Bringing your children to recording sessions will ruin both their childhood and the band
- If you have to reform, don't make a new album

SUMMARY

SO WHAT HAVE WE LEARNED OVERALL?

Well, the plan for forming a perfect band, and keeping it that way—
the complete guide to avoiding bandalism.

It's actually quite simple:
- Find the right members so that it feels exciting.
- Make sure you're all playing the right instruments to fit your personalities.
- Get to know each other properly.
- Let the music you want to make tell you how to write it.
- Find an image that makes you feel like a gang (and, with any luck, keeps everyone in their place) and a name that isn't too lame.
- Build an industry igloo around yourselves to shelter from corrosive commerce.
- Use tantrums in the studio if nothing else will get you heard.

- Don't say stupid things to the press or believe a word that gets written about you.
- Don't sell your songs for gasoline commercials if all your interviews are about the evils of global warming.
- Keep your sanity on tour and avoid nervous exhaustion.
- Check into rehab or at least ring your mom before you even think about writing the second album.
- Don't fire anyone unless they're actually trying to kill you.
- Do anything you can to fix a feud.
- Don't make a second album about being in a band or within a year you'll be on unemployment.
- Keep revitalizing yourselves on the album-tour treadmill with new records and new trousers until you've all got kids or the drummer dies.
- Don't split up the band until you've stopped being good or it's genuinely more miserable than having a proper job.
- Never reform without special dispensation from God.

And that's it. You formed a perfect band, kept it brilliant, and broke up at just the right time to leave a lasting impression, an enviable back-catalog, and a world changed for the better in your wake.

You're cool forever, well before your fortieth birthday . . .

. . . until, against all the advice I've given, you can't resist the temptation to reform. And then you will have to read this book all over again. (*See preface, p. xiii.*)

THE BANDALISM HELP DESK

Any bandalism tales of your own? Of ludicrous fallings out, ego-ridden musical disasters, or guitar-throwing tantrums? We'd love to hear them (we're gluttons for excruciating band misery).
If so, e-mail us your stories at:

http://www.myspace.com/bandalismthebook

Or do you just need a solution to your own band's bandalistic tendencies? Julian Ridgway will suggest remedies for the best queries and post them on the page, with your anonymity intact if you prefer, to try to help you get your band back in order.